Cambridge English

Complete IELTS

Bands 5–6.5

Teacher's Book

**Guy Brook-Hart and Vanessa Jakeman
with David Jay**

CAMBRIDGE
UNIVERSITY PRESS

CAMBRIDGE UNIVERSITY PRESS
Cambridge, New York, Melbourne, Madrid, Cape Town,
Singapore, São Paulo, Delhi, Tokyo, Mexico City

Cambridge University Press
The Edinburgh Building, Cambridge CB2 8RU, UK

www.cambridge.org
Information on this title: www.cambridge.org/9780521185165

First published 2012

Printed in China by Golden Cup Printing Co. Ltd

A catalogue record for this publication is available from the British Library

ISBN 978-0-521-17948-5 Student's Book with Answers with CD-ROM
ISBN 978-0-521-17949-2 Student's Book without Answers with CD-ROM
ISBN 978-0-521-18516-5 Teacher's Book
ISBN 978-0521-17950-8 Class Audio CDs (2)
ISBN 978-0521-17953-9 Student's Book Pack (Student's Book with Answers with CD-ROM
and Class Audio CDs (2))
ISBN 978-1107-40197-6 Workbook with Answers with Audio CD
ISBN 978-1107-40196-9 Workbook without Answers with Audio CD

Contents

Introduction

Who Complete IELTS is for

Complete IELTS is an enjoyable and motivating topic-based course designed to give thorough preparation for the IELTS test. It offers:

- comprehensive analysis and practice of the **task types** used in IELTS Reading, Listening, Speaking and Writing papers.
- a step-by-step approach to **writing tasks** using models as guidance and sample answers.
- a systematic approach to **speaking tasks** with model answers and a focus on pronunciation.
- stimulating authentic reading texts that provide training in the skills and strategies needed to deal with exam **reading tasks**.
- listening activities that provide training in the skills and strategies needed to deal with exam **listening tasks**.
- coverage of major **grammar** and **vocabulary** areas which are known to be essential for success in IELTS. These are supported by work on correcting common mistakes as revealed in the Cambridge Learner Corpus.
- motivating **pair work** and **group work** exercises.

What the Student's Book contains

- **Eight topic-based units of nine pages** each covering topic areas frequently encountered in IELTS.
- Each unit covers tasks from each of the four papers in the exam, so all units contain work on **Listening**, **Reading**, **Writing** and **Speaking**. The units also cover **essential IELTS-related grammar and vocabulary**.
- Each exam task type is integrated into a range of classroom activities designed to equip students with the **strategies and approaches** needed to deal with the demands of IELTS.
- Practice for each part of the test is accompanied by **detailed information and advice** about what the task involves and how best to approach it.
- **Eight unit reviews** that provide additional exercises on the grammar and vocabulary encountered in each unit.

- **Writing and Speaking Reference sections** containing detailed advice to students on how to approach writing and speaking tasks in the exam, complete with exercises and model answers.
- A **Language Reference section** giving clear and detailed explanations of the grammar covered in each unit.
- **Eight Word Lists** containing lexical items encountered in the Student's Book units or recording scripts.

  We suggest that the best time to use these lists is towards the end of the unit, perhaps before doing the Speaking or the Writing sections. Students may use these lists for self-study and reinforcement of lexis encountered in the unit. Here are some suggestions as to how students can use them which you can discuss with them.

  - Students should use the page reference given to find the items in the unit and study how the words/phrases are used in context.

  - They can use a learner's dictionary (such as CALD) to compare the dictionary definitions with the definitions given in the word list. In many cases the definitions will coincide, but they will be able to study further examples in the dictionary.

  - Students can annotate the word lists themselves or copy items to their notebooks for further study.

  - You can suggest to students that they should not try to memorise all the items, but they should select a number of words and phrases that seem most useful to them and try to use them when doing speaking and writing tasks.

- A **full IELTS Practice Test**.
- A **CD-ROM intended for self-study** which provides further exercises to prepare students for IELTS.

The Cambridge Learner Corpus (CLC) ⊘

The Cambridge Learner Corpus (CLC) is a large collection of exam scripts written by students taking Cambridge ESOL English exams around the world. It contains over 200,000 scripts and is growing all the time. It forms part of the Cambridge International Corpus (CIC) and it has been built up by Cambridge University Press and Cambridge ESOL. The CLC contains scripts from:

- 200,000 students.
- 100 different first languages.
- 180 different countries.

Exercises in the Student's Book which are based on the CLC are indicated by the following icon. ☉

What the Workbook contains

- **Eight units designed for homework and self-study**. Each unit contains full exam practice of **IELTS Reading** and **Listening tasks**.
- **IELTS writing tasks** with model answers.
- Further practice in the **grammar** and **vocabulary** taught in the Student's Book.
- An **audio CD** containing all the listening material for the Workbook.

What the Teacher's Book contains

- **Detailed notes** for the eight units in the Student's Book which:
  - state the **objectives** of each unit.
  - give **step-by-step advice** on how to treat each part of each Student's Book unit.
  - give **supporting information** to teachers and students about IELTS tasks.
  - offer suggestions for **alternative treatments** of the materials in the Student's Book.
  - offer a wide range of ideas for **extension activities** to follow up Student's Book activities.
  - contain **comprehensive answer keys** for each activity and exercise, including suggested answers where appropriate.
- **Eight photocopiable activities**, one for each unit, designed to provide enjoyable recycling of work done in the Student's Book unit, but without a specific exam focus. All photocopiable activities are accompanied by teacher's notes outlining:
  - the objectives of the activity.
  - a suggested procedure for handling the activity in the classroom.

- **Four photocopiable Progress Tests**, one for every two units, to test grammar and vocabulary taught in the units.
- **Eight photocopiable Vocabulary Extension word lists.**

The words and phrases in the photocopiable Vocabulary Extension word lists have been selected using the Cambridge International Corpus and relate to the topics of the unit. They are intended to provide students with extra vocabulary when doing IELTS tasks.

We suggest that you hand these lists out near the beginning of the unit. Most of the words and phrases do not occur in the units themselves, but students may be able to use some of them during the speaking or writing activities in the unit. Here are some suggestions on how these word lists can be used:

- Ask students to go through the word lists in conjunction with a good learner's dictionary such as CALD and check how the words/phrases are used in the examples (many of the definitions will be the same).
- Ask students to select 5–10 items which they would like to be able to use themselves and ask them to write their own sentences using the items.
- Encourage students to copy the items they find most useful to their notebooks.
- Ask students to refer to these word lists before doing speaking or writing tasks in the units. Give students time to look at the relevant list and think (and discuss with you) how they can use words/phrases before they do the task itself.
- When students do the tasks, pay particular attention to any use they make of items from the lists and give them feedback on how correctly they have used an item.

What the Class Audio CDs contain

There are **two audio CDs** containing **listening and speaking material** for the eight units of the Student's Book plus the Listening Practice Test. The listening and speaking materials are indicated by different coloured icons for each of the CDs.

Unit 1 Starting somewhere new

Unit objectives

- **Listening Section 1:** introduction to form-completion tasks and multiple-choice tasks
- **Reading Section 1:** skimming; introduction to True / False / Not Given and table-completion tasks
- **Vocabulary:** *problem* or *trouble*; *affect* or *effect*; *percent* or *percentage*
- **Speaking Part 1:** how to answer Part 1 questions at length; giving reasons, extra details and using their own words (not the examiner's) when answering the question
- **Pronunciation:** sentence stress – stressing content words
- **Writing Task 1:** different types of graphic for presenting information; introductory sentences; interpreting graphics; structuring the summary; basic planning
- **Key grammar:** making comparisons – comparison of adjectives and adverbs

Starting off

❶ *As a warmer*

- For students to get to know each other, with books closed, write on the board:

  Find out who ...

  – *... has travelled furthest to come to this class.*

  – *... has lived in another country for longest.*

  – *... has the most interesting reason for doing the IELTS test.*

- Tell students they will have to ask other students questions to find out this information.

- Elicit possible questions, e.g. *How far have you travelled to come to this class? How long have you lived in another country? Why are you doing / going to do the IELTS test?*

- Ask students to walk around the class and talk to three students who are not sitting next to them. When they have finished, ask them to work in pairs and compare their answers with the questions on the board.

- Round up with the whole class and elicit details of the student who has travelled furthest, etc.

Alternative treatment With reasons a–d covered, ask students to work in pairs, look at the photos and decide what aspect of studying abroad each photo shows. Students then uncover the reasons and compare them with their own ideas.

> **Answers**
> **a** 2   **b** 1   **c** 4   **d** 3

❷ Ask students to discuss these two questions in pairs or small groups.

Listening   Section 1

❶

> **Suggested answer**
> An international social club is a place for people of different nationalities to meet.

Extension idea Ask students: *How could you benefit from studying/socialising with people from different countries?*

❷

> Draw students' attention to the Exam overview in the Student's Book on page 7. Point out that in the IELTS exam, they hear each part once only, so it's important to know what to expect before listening. Also mention that students should write their answers in the question booklet while the recording is playing. They then have 10 minutes to transfer them onto an answer sheet at the end of the test. This means they can underline things in the question booklet as they do the test, but they need to make sure they can read their answers later on.
>
> Form-completion tasks test students' ability to listen for specific details: it's important to know what details to listen for beforehand.

Ask students to look at Questions 1–5. Explain that the recording is always broken into two sections in Part 1 and that they have some time to read the questions first. Elicit the type of answers that each question will need (*suggested answers:* 1 a nationality 2 a house number and street name 3 a phone number 4 a job or occupation 5 a free-time activity).

Extension idea To make sure students know the names of letters and numbers, write some names and numbers on the board. Ask students to spell them, or read out the numbers. Ask students to work in pairs and spell the names of friends to each other. The student who listens should write them down.

If there is time, they could also dictate some memorable dates, important times, number sequences, etc. to each other.

❸ Play the recording once and ask students to check their answers together in pairs. If necessary, play the recording again, but explain that this would not be possible in the exam.

> **Answers**
> **1** Malaysian   **2** 13 Anglesea   **3** 040 422 9160
> **4** economist   **5** dancing

❹ Tell students that they will have some time to read Questions 6–10 as well, which they should use to underline the key idea in each question. Explain that the questions also help to guide their listening; for example, Question 6 refers to a problem, so students can expect the start of the second part of the recording to mention something in relation to a problem (*suggested underlining*: 6 problem; 7 How many members; 8 How often; 9 most frequent type of activity; 10 purpose).

❺ Tell students that because they listen only once, they should choose their answers while they are listening. In the exam there will be a short pause at the end of Listening Section 1 and then Listening Section 2 starts. If your students need extra help, play the recording a second time so they can check their answers.

> **Answers**
> **6** C (you might find some of our Australian slang more difficult to understand)   **7** B (currently about 50 members)   **8** B (every second Thursday)
> **9** A (usually one of the members gives a little presentation)   **10** A (the main point of the club is to give people like you the chance to mix in more with people from this country)

❻ Before they start, ask students to work in pairs and think of possible questions to ask, then elicit from the whole class. (*Suggested questions:* What's your name? How old are you? What nationality are you? Where do you live / are you living? Can you give me your mobile phone number? What do you do / What is your occupation? What do you enjoy doing in your free time?)

Suggest to students that they ask extra follow-up questions to make the activity more of a conversation.

Reading   Section 1

❶ *As a warmer* If appropriate with your class, ask students these questions.

*   *Do people from other countries come to study or work in your country?*

*   *What sort of things do they study? What work do they do?*

*   *Do they have any problems when they first arrive? If so, what problems?*

Ask students to discuss the list in the book. Encourage them to talk from their experiences or about people they know.

❷

> Draw students' attention again to the Exam overview in the Student's Book on page 7. Elicit that the Reading Paper has three sections, each taking approximately 20 minutes. Point out that whereas in the Listening Paper they have time at the end to transfer their answers to the answer sheet, in the Reading Paper they do this while they are reading (i.e. they don't have extra time). Give students the following information.
>
> *   In the exam, they will have about 20 minutes for each section of the Reading Paper, but that in class they are going to practise skills and techniques for more effective reading, so things will probably take longer.
>
> *   IELTS Reading passages will usually have a title and often a subheading. They should pay attention to these before they start reading as this will help orientate them through the text.

Ask students to discuss their answers to the question in pairs, then round up with the whole class. (*Suggested answer*: The experience and problems of going to live in a different culture.)

Tell students to glance quickly at the passage and the tasks which follow so they have an idea before they start of how much they will have to read and what they will have to do while reading.

❸ Explain to students that the purpose of this question is to practise skimming the passage to get a general idea of its content before reading it more carefully (skimming is reading quickly and superficially to get a general idea of the content and structure of a passage without trying to understand in detail or deal with difficult vocabulary or concepts).

Give students three minutes to do this. Be strict with the time limit. Tell them that they should not try to understand every word and every sentence.

Answer
The second stage.

Extension idea Tell students: *The passage seems to have two parts. What is each part about?* (*Answer*: The first part is about Australian culture; the second part is about the stages of culture shock.)

❹ Tell students that the True / False / Not Given task is often found in Reading Section 1. It is designed to see whether they can correctly identify information that is in the text and identify whether information is expressed in the text or not.

• Point out that this first exercise illustrates the difference between the three options. Ask students to look at the passage printed in blue and then to discuss their answers in pairs.

Answers
1 TRUE   **2** NOT GIVEN   **3** FALSE

• Elicit reasons for each answer by asking students to quote from the passage (1 most people – *almost everyone* – TRUE; 2 there is no comparison of different types of people – NOT GIVEN; 3 only affects how people feel – *physical and emotional discomfort* – FALSE).

It is often difficult to decide if a question is FALSE or NOT GIVEN. Students should choose FALSE when the information in the passage contradicts the statement. They should choose NOT GIVEN when there is no information about the statement in the passage.

❺ This task tests students' ability to scan the passage to locate the right place and then to read that part of the passage in detail to find the answer (scanning is when you read quickly to locate specific information in a passage).

• Tell students that the questions in True / False / Not Given tasks usually contain a word or phrase which is the same or similar to a word or phrase in the passage. This is to help them locate the part of the passage which relates to the statement, even when detailed reading shows the answer to be NOT GIVEN.

• Ask students to scan the passage to find words and phrases similar to the underlined words and phrases in Questions 1–6 and then to read those parts of the passage to answer the questions. (Question 1 mentions teachers. Therefore, students should scan till they find *teachers* or *course tutors* in the passage and read that section carefully.)

• When students have answered the questions, elicit the evidence in the passage which gives them their answers (given in brackets in the key).

Answers
1 TRUE (… *a teacher or course tutor will not tell students what to do but will give them a number of options and suggest they work out which one is the best* …)
2 NOT GIVEN (There is a reference to *teachers*, *students* and *circumstances* but no mention of whether teachers show an interest in students' personal circumstances.)
3 TRUE (… *Australians are uncomfortable with differences in status and hence idealise the idea of treating everyone equally. An illustration of this is that most adult Australians call each other by their first names.*)
4 FALSE (… *some students may be critical of others who they perceive as doing nothing but study.*)
5 FALSE (*Australian notions of privacy mean that areas such as financial matters, appearance and relationships are only discussed with close friends.*)
6 NOT GIVEN (There is mention of *Australians*, *friendship* and *older people* but no comparison is made regarding how friendly young and old people are).

❻ This task tests students' ability to scan for information using words already in the table to help them locate answers.

• Ask students to read the rubric and check how many words they can write in each space. Explain that *NO MORE THAN TWO* means one or two at the most. If they write three words – even if the answer is among those words – they will lose the mark for the question.

• Tell students that it is important to look at the task to see what part of the passage they need to read again in order to answer the questions: they don't always need to read everything again.

Answers
1 No (the parts describing the stages)
2 Nouns / noun phrases.
3 **7** the name of a stage   **8** something like a connection   **9** a length of time   **10** a feeling   **11** something you can observe   **12** something for dealing with difficulties   **13** the name of a stage

7 To get students started, give Question 7 as an example. Ask students to scan to find *honeymoon* in the passage. Elicit why this is the correct answer to Question 7 (*the first stage ... often referred to as the "honeymoon" stage*). Elicit why *honeymoon* is in inverted commas. (*Answer:* because *honeymoon* normally refers to the holiday or trip two people make at the beginning of a marriage, when everything in their relationship appears to be perfect).

- Ask students which words they will use to help them find the answers to the other questions. Tell students to underline the words they need for their answers in the passage and then copy them to the spaces provided. Many students lose marks because they copy words wrongly or add unnecessary words.

> **Answers**
> **7** Honeymoon **8** similarities **9** a/one month
> **10** enthusiasm **11** (cutural) clues
> **12** (problem-solving) skills **13** Adaptation

Extension idea Write some of your students' 'wrong' answers on the board and discuss why they are wrong.

8 Ask students to prepare by thinking and making notes for two or three minutes before they discuss. Help individuals with any vocabulary they need.

Alternative treatment If you have students from the same country, ask them to work in pairs and prepare a short talk to answer the second question. When they are ready, they change partners and take turns to give their talk.

Vocabulary

Problem or *trouble*? *Affect* or *effect*?

1 After students have read the dictionary extracts, check understanding by asking questions such as the following.

- *Which word, 'trouble' or 'problem', can you make plural?* (*Answer: problems*)
- *Which doesn't use the word 'a' before it?* (*Answer: trouble*)
- *Which word would you use when talking about a difficulty you want to work on or solve?* (*Answer: problem*)
- *Which word might you use for something which worries you but you won't take any action?* (*Answer: trouble*)
- *Which word is a noun and which is a verb: 'affect' or 'effect'?* (*Answer:* noun – *effect*; verb – *affect*)
- Use the example in Question 1 to ask: *Why is 'problems' correct?* (*Answer: trouble* is uncountable and not used before *a*).

- When students have done the exercise, elicit why each answer is correct.

> **Answers**
> **2** problem
> **3** affect
> **4** effect

2 Tell students all the mistakes in this exercise were made by IELTS candidates doing the Writing Paper; they should avoid mistakes with these words when writing.

> Answers
> **2** ✓ **3** ~~affect~~ effect **4** ~~effect~~ affect **5** ~~affect~~ effect **6** ~~troubles~~ problems

Speaking Part 1

1 🎧 ***As a warmer*** With books closed, ask students to work in small groups.

- Ask: *Have you ever done a speaking test in a foreign language? If so, what was it like?*
- Tell students to work in small groups. In their notebooks, they write a list of advice to give candidates going to do a speaking test (e.g. speak clearly so the examiner can hear you).

Again, refer students to the Exam overview in the Student's Book on page 7. Elicit how long the Speaking test lasts, how many parts it has, and that there is one examiner and one candidate only. Point out that there is a short introduction at the start of the test and this is not assessed.

Give students time to look at the ten questions in Exercise 1. Explain that in part 1, they will be asked straightforward questions about themselves. There are always two groups of questions on familiar topics, e.g. travelling or where you live. Suggest that they use Part 1 to get warmed up and start feeling confident about talking in English. Then play the recording. (The recordings in these Speaking practice sections are not intended as listening comprehension exercises, but as models for students to get ideas from or imitate.)

> **Answers**
> **b** 9 **c** 4 **d** 2

2 To get students started, elicit why statement 1 is not a good idea. (*Suggested answer:* The examiner wants to hear how well you speak, your use of grammar, pronunciation over whole sentences, how well you structure your answer, etc., and can't do this if you answer with two or three words).

Ask students to give reasons for their answers.

> **Answers**
> 1 – 2 ✓ 3 ✓ 4 ✓ 5 – 6 ✓

❸ 🎧

> **Answers**
> They all do 2, 3, 4 and 6.

Note: This is a good moment to do the work in the Pronunciation section on sentence stress, which is based on the four students' answers.

❹ *Extension idea* Tell students you are going to think about body language in the Speaking paper. Write the following on the board and ask students if they are good things to do.

- *smile when you enter the room*
- *say good morning/afternoon/evening*
- *look at the table or the ceiling when answering questions*
- *sit forward and look interested*

Some of these may depend on your students' cultural background, but generally we would expect students to smile, look at the examiner when answering a question, and to look interested.

❺ Tell students to ask each other questions 1–10 from Exercise 1. The student who is interviewing can keep a checklist of the things written on the board, and those mentioned in Exercise 2. They should give their partner feedback on these things.

Extension idea When they have finished, ask students to change partners and do the exercise again, concentrating on correct sentence stress.

Pronunciation
Sentence stress 1

❶ 🎧 Elicit what types of words are underlined in extract 1 (*Answer*: nouns and adjectives). Point out to students that the words which give information in answer to the question are likely to be stressed.

Remind students that Pronunciation counts for a quarter of their IELTS score. This means that in addition to listening to their grammar, vocabulary and fluency, examiners also note how easily they can understand the candidate: candidates who speak too fast/slowly or mutter will lose marks for pronunciation; those who speak clearly and at the correct pace will do better.

Explain that there are recognised features of pronunciation, and examiners want to see how well candidates can use and control these. Sentence stress is one of these features, along with things like

intonation, rhythm and the pronunciation of sounds. If they stress the wrong words or too many words in a sentence, it can significantly affect the meaning, or candidates may sound very odd. If they stress the right words, it will help the listener understand them.

Alternative treatment Before listening to extracts 2–4, play extract 1, and ask students how stressed words are different from unstressed words. Ask:

- *Does the speaker say them louder? (Answer:* no)
- *Does the speaker take longer to say them, pronouncing them more clearly? (Answer:* yes)

Then ask students to look at extracts 2–4 and predict which words will be stressed. They then listen and check their answers.

> **Suggested answers**
> 2 Well, I'm not <u>too</u> keen on <u>flying</u> because you spend too <u>long</u> at <u>airports</u>.
> 3 I find it <u>hard</u> being away from my <u>family</u> and <u>not</u> <u>seeing</u> my <u>friends</u>.
> 4 I've <u>been</u> here since I <u>came</u> to <u>university</u>, so for about <u>two</u> <u>years</u>.

❷ *Alternative treatment* If your students need, drill them by reading the sentences yourself and asking individual students to repeat.

Writing Task 1

❶ Before doing the warmer, refer students to the Exam 0verview on page 7 and elicit:

- how long the Writing paper takes.
- how many tasks they will have to do and what each consists of.
- how long they should spend on each task.

As a warmer Ask students to look at the different ways of displaying information in this exercise. Tell them that these are the sort of diagrams and charts they will see in the exam. Ask:

- *Where might you expect to see diagrams and charts like these? (Suggested answer*: in a textbook or an academic article)
- *Why are diagrams and charts often used to display information? (Suggested answer*: They provide a clear illustration of comparisons, trends, processes, etc., and are easier for people with a visual intelligence).

> **Answers**
> 2 D 3 C 4 A 5 E

❷ Students often find writing the first sentence hard. A good way to start is by saying the type of graphic, its purpose and the time period (if any) or the main items mentioned. Point out that students should use their own words where possible – copying phrases from the question does not show language ability and may be penalised when the examiner counts the words.

> **Answers**
> 1 the graph
> 2 shows the changes in the number of people from abroad who visited Townsville, Queensland
> 3 over a four-year period

❸

> **Answers**
> B The chart shows the number of households in Winchester, California, and the languages which people speak there.
> C The chart shows the difficulties people have when they integrate into a new country and how the problems vary according to age.

❹ Ask students to work in pairs and to use their own words.

> **Suggested answers**
> D The diagram shows a machine for producing electricity from waves.
> E The table shows the number of students at Broadlands Language School and the average number of weeks each student spent there over a three-month period.

❺ As this is the first time in this course that students will see a full task, draw attention to the rubric. Highlight the words *Summarise* and *comparisons* and elicit how they should write their answers (formal, academic, continuous prose) and what they should include (similarities and differences).

> **Suggested answers**
> 1 Their biggest problem is making friends (46%); this is higher than for the middle age group (36%) and the oldest age group (23%).
> 2 Learning the local language is most problematic for the oldest age group – 54% compared with 29% for the youngest.
> 3 The oldest age group has the least difficulty with finding somewhere to live (22%), compared with 39% for the middle age group and 40% for the youngest.

❻ Tell students to compare the information in the sample answer with the information on the chart. Are all the important details covered? Is there anything significant/important missing? Has the writer changed the words or used the same ones as in the question?

> **Answers**
> 1 Question 1: paragraph 2
>   Question 2: paragraph 3
>   Question 3: paragraph 4
> 2 To give a general overview of all the information.

Note This would be a good moment to refer students to the Writing reference on page 92.

❼

> **Answers**
> 1 b move to   c a new country
> 2 How the problems vary according to people's ages

❽ Tell students to pay special attention when using these words in the IELTS test.

> **Answers**
> 1 *percent*   2 *percentage*   3 no   4 *the*   5 no

❾

> **Answers**
> 2 ...and **the** percentage of people in prison...
> 3 ...to ~~a~~ two percent.
> 4 ...approximately 58 ~~percents~~ percent...
> 5 ...that **the** percentage...
> 6 ...to 25 ~~percentage~~ percent...

Extension idea Ask students to write two or three sentences using *percent* and *percentage* based on Chart B in Exercise 1 and then compare their sentences.

Note This is a good moment to do the work in Key grammar on page 16.

Suggested answer

1 The chart shows some of the problems people have when they go abroad, by age group.

2 (see 1)

3 Their biggest problem is sorting out health care; 37% have this problem compared with 36% of the older age group and 32% of the younger age group.

4 The middle age group has the most problems related to money (35%), compared with 34% of 18- to 34-year-olds and 29% of 55-year-olds and over.

5 The middle age group has the most and the oldest age group the least.

6 The middle age group.

11 This Writing task is probably best done for homework. Although students will have approximately 20 minutes for this in the exam, it is reasonable to suggest that they take a little longer at this stage in the course.

Suggested answers

The chart shows three areas of difficulty people have when they move to another country and how these difficulties vary according to age.

The greatest problem for people of all ages is arranging medical care. Between 32 and 37 percent of all people find this a problem.

The second biggest problem is organising finances. Although only 29 percent of people over 55 are affected by this, 35 percent of the middle age group and 34 percent of the 18–34 age group experience difficulties in this area.

In contrast, fewer people have difficulties with education. While 19 percent of the 35–54 age group have trouble finding a suitable school for their children, the percentage of people in the other two age groups is much lower at 6 percent for the young age group and 3 percent for the over 55s.

In general, all people experience problems to some extent. However, the percentage of the 35-54 age group who find their new arrangements difficult is slightly higher than the others, particularly in relation to education.

(177 words)

Extension idea

- Set a deadline for doing the task. When students bring their completed summary to class, ask them to exchange it with a partner and each draw a bar chart based on the information in their partner's

answer. They then compare their charts and look for differences between their charts and the one in the Student's Book.

- Tell them to check their partner's answer to see if they have used language for making comparisons correctly and *percent* and *percentage* correctly. Ask students to feed back to their partners and make any corrections which are necessary. Round up any problems with the whole class before students hand their work to you.

Key grammar
Making comparisons

1 After students have done the exercise, go through the rules in the Language reference on page 100.

Answers
b 1   **c** 2   **d** 4

Answers
2 harder   3 friendlier / more friendly
4 warmer; colder   5 Older; better

Answers
2 ~~better~~ best
3 ~~more clean and safe~~ cleaner and safer
4 The ~~most~~ highest
5 ~~worser~~ worse
6 ~~more well~~ better

Unit 1 photocopiable activity:
Study buddies

Time: 30-40 minutes

Objectives
- To help students to get to know each other better
- To practise talking about cultural experiences and language-learning preferences
- To answer questions on personal topics, giving reasons and extra details
- To practise making comparisons
- To practise structuring and preparing a summary

Before class

You will need one photocopy of the activity page on page 14 for each student.

In class

1 *As a warmer* Ask students: *Have you ever been on a study trip with your school or university? If so, was it a positive or negative experience? Why?*

Hand out one activity page to each student. Ask them to do Exercise 1 alone. When students have read the email and answered the questions, check answers with the class.

Suggested answers
1 To give her students more information about the upcoming study trip to Edinburgh.
2 To help students get to know the partner they will be working with on the trip.

2 Students do the questionnaire alone, choosing the option which best matches their own answers to each question. Encourage them to think of reasons and extra details to support each choice. Explain that it is not a problem if more than one option is true for them or if they have other answers, but they should be prepared to give reasons for their answers. Students compare answers in pairs. They should give their reasons for each choice.

- Encourage them to ask follow-up questions to find out more about their partner. *Why do you prefer ...? Why don't you like ...?*

- Ask each pair to prepare a short presentation (the summary should last a maximum of three minutes) summarising what they have found out about each other from the questionnaire. Encourage students to write notes, not the whole summary. They should include comparisons about the following: travel experience; dealing with new cultures; study habits; social life. Elicit a basic structure for their presentation (introductory sentence – similarities – differences – conclusion).

Remind them to use language for making comparisons taught in Unit 1, for example: *Omar finds speaking in seminars easier than I do, but he's less independent when travelling.*

- Ask students to take turns to present their summaries to the whole class. At the end of each presentation, the rest of the class should say briefly whether they think each pair will make good study partners or not. Encourage them to give reasons.

Extension idea As students are giving their presentations, monitor for any errors they make, particularly with language for making comparisons. To do this, you could note down a few typical errors during the presentations, without identifying the students who made them. In the next session, distribute copies of an error sheet for students to correct in pairs or groups. After they have discussed the errors, write the correct versions on the board.

Unit 1 photocopiable activity
Study buddies

1 Read this email from your college tutor. Then answer the questions.

1 What is Alison's main reason for writing?

2 What is the purpose of the questionnaire?

2 Look at Alison's questionnaire below. Tick the option (A, B or C) you most agree with. Then compare your answers with a partner.

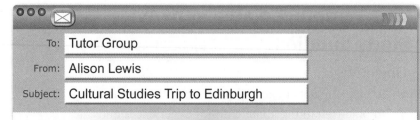

To: Tutor Group

From: Alison Lewis

Subject: Cultural Studies Trip to Edinburgh

Dear all,

Several of you have emailed me asking for more information about the Cultural Studies Research Trip to Edinburgh next month.

This is to let you know that on the trip you will be working together and sharing accommodation with one other student. The attached questionnaire should help you to find out more about your study partner, to see if you will feel able to travel and work together.

During the trip, you will be able to attend lectures and seminars with local university students, as well as visit historic buildings and places of interest. I will email you again next week with a detailed schedule. In the meantime, please let me know if you have any questions.

Best wishes,

Alison

---

1 How much experience do you have of travelling abroad?

A I have travelled a lot and feel confident in most situations.

B I have some experience of dealing with new situations.

C I haven't travelled much.

2 What kind of traveller are you?

A I'm independent and like visiting places alone.

B I'm happy to travel alone but I prefer to have company.

C I prefer to be part of a group.

3 What is the best way to learn about another country's culture?

A Read as much about the country as possible.

B Visit the most famous cultural sites and decide for myself.

C Spend time talking to local people.

4 How do you feel about meeting people from other cultures?

A It's easy for me, and I really enjoy it.

B I feel nervous at first, but then I manage fine.

C It takes quite a long time for me to get to know people.

5 How do you feel about doing research?

A I prefer to work independently.

B I sometimes like working with a study partner.

C I prefer working with others.

6 In seminars and group discussions

A I speak when I feel I have something important to say.

B I don't usually speak, unless somebody asks me to.

C I usually talk a lot.

7 When someone has different opinions from mine

A I usually tell them immediately that I disagree.

B I change the topic without giving my opinion.

C I pretend to agree with them, in order to be polite.

8 In college accommodation

A I am always very tidy and organised.

B I am organised, but it depends on my mood.

C I prefer not to tidy up myself.

9 When I'm studying

A I need to have the TV on or music playing all the time.

B I need complete silence most of the time.

C I study quietly but take breaks to chat or watch TV.

10 After a busy day on a study trip, I would like to

A go out and socialise with other students.

B chat on the Internet to friends and family at home.

C write about the experiences I had during the day.

Vocabulary extension

Unit 1

Abbreviations: n/pln = noun / plural noun; v = verb; adj = adjective; adv = adverb; p = phrase;
T/I = transitive/intransitive; C/U = countable/uncountable

adapt to a new culture p to change your way of life to fit in with the customs and beliefs in a new place

association n [C] an organisation of people with the same interests or with a particular purpose

become a member p If you become a member of a club or organisation, you join it.

capital city n [U] the most important city in a country or state, where the government is based

club event n [C] an activity, competition, party, etc. that has been organised by a club

commercial district n [C] an area of a city where there are a lot of businesses

cosmopolitan atmosphere n [U] If a place has a cosmopolitan atmosphere, there are people and things from many countries and cultures in it.

debating society n [C] a club where speakers argue against each other about subjects in a formal way

from diverse backgrounds p If people are from diverse backgrounds, they are very different from each other, for example in race, education or wealth.

emigrant n [C] someone who leaves their own country to go and live in another one

immigration rules pln [C] rules or laws connected with coming to live in another country

in the city centre p in the central area of a city, where there are a lot of shops

in the suburbs p in one of the areas at the edge of a town or city where people who work in the town or city often live

industrial city n [C] a city that has a lot of industry and factories

integrate into the community p to mix with and join in with the customs of a group of people

live on the outskirts p to live in one of the areas of housing on the edge of a town or city

local culture n [U] the customs, beliefs and way of life of a particular area

member of a club n [C] If you are a member of a club, you belong to that club.

multicultural society n [U] a society that includes people with many different customs and beliefs

on the coast p in an area near the sea

overcome one's culture shock p to succeed in becoming accustomed to a culture that is very different from your own

small village p a very small town in the countryside

to experience something new p If you experience something new, it happens to you or you feel it for the first time.

to respect other peoples' attitudes p to accept and be polite about other people's beliefs and opinions

long tradition n [U] something that a society or other group of people has been doing for a long time

wealthy neighbourhood n [C] an area of a town or city where rich people live

youth club n [C] a place where young people can go to meet other young people and do social activities

Unit 2 It's good for you!

Unit objectives

- **Reading Section 2:** introduction to matching headings, and 'pick from a list' tasks; work on skimming
- **Listening Section 2:** introduction to labelling a map task; further work on multiple choice
- **Vocabulary:** word formation
- **Speaking Part 2:** using the prompt; making notes before speaking; using discourse markers to structure the talk
- **Pronunciation:** introduction to intonation
- **Writing Part 2:** analysing tasks with two questions to address; using linking words and phrases; planning an essay
- **Key grammar:** countable and uncountable nouns

Starting off

1 *As a warmer* With books closed, ask students to work in small groups and tell each other about three things they eat which are healthy and three things they eat which are not so healthy.

They then open their books and discuss which of the photos relate to healthy food and which to unhealthy food.

> **Answers**
> 1 battery farming   2 pesticide use
> 3 outdoor farming   4 natural fertiliser
> 5 crop rotation   6 genetic engineering

2

> **Suggested answers**
> 1 Organic vegetables and fruit are grown using natural fertiliser and soil. Organic meat is farmed outdoors where the animals are reared in a healthy environment with plenty of space.
> 3 Photos 3, 4 and 5

Reading   Section 2

1 Remind students that the title and subheading are there to help them do the task. The title will give them the topic of the passage and the subheading will tell them what aspect of the topic is going to be covered.

> **Suggested answer**
> The last sentence of the subheading suggests that the writers are going to question whether organic food is better for the environment and for people's health. So this passage is likely to contain some arguments by the writers and it is useful to try and understand these arguments, as they form part of an overview of the passage.

2

> **Answers**
> The writers are against organic food.

3 The aim of the matching headings task is to test students' ability to identify the main idea or purpose of each paragraph. Tell students that when questions are printed before the passage, they should read the questions carefully before reading the passage, so they know what they are looking for when they start reading and they save time. Ask students to compare what they have underlined with a partner, then round up with the whole class.

> **Suggested underlining**
> **i** research / organic food / better for us
> **ii** Adding up / cost / organic food
> **iii** factors / affect food quality
> **iv** rich and poor / differently
> **v** description / organic farming
> **vi** Testing / taste / organic food
> **vii** Fear / science / created / organic trend
> **ix** hidden dangers / food

4 *Alternative treatment*

- Before doing this task, give students practice in skimming by saying: *You have three minutes to quickly read this article and get a general idea of what it's about. Find out if the writers are in favour of organic food or against it.* (*Answer:* against)

- Ask students to work in pairs and look at the underlined sentences in paragraph A. Ask students why heading viii is the correct answer for A. (*Answer:* Paragraph A addresses heading viii – organic food is popular because people feel it is more 'natural'.) Compare *the main reason* and *the popularity of organic food* in the heading with *the attraction of organic food* and *the really important thing* in paragraph A.

Note: Another way of expressing heading viii is *What is the main reason for the popularity of organic food?*, which matches the passage very closely.

- Tell students that the headings for paragraphs B and C are either i or v. Ask them to decide which is which and why. (*Answers*: B v C i)

- Tell students to work alone and finish the exercise. Give them a maximum of seven minutes to do this. Remind them that there are more headings than paragraphs, so they will not need them all.

Answers
2 v   3 i   4 iii   5 ix   6 vii   7 iv

- After going through the answers, point out that headings ii and vi do not fit any of the paragraphs because there is nothing in the passage about the key ideas they express (ii Adding up / cost / organic food; and vi Testing / taste / organic food).

Extension idea Draw students' attention to how they have just followed the procedure in the Exam advice.

❺ The aim of the 'pick from a list' task is to scan the passage to find the relevant section(s) and then read those sections in detail to answer the question. (*Suggested underlining*: Questions 8–9 – mention / connection / organic farming; options – A use of pesticides, B same field / different crops, C soil quality, D reducing / farm workers, E greenhouse gases; Questions 10–11 – factors / affect / nutritional content of food; options – A who prepares, B weather / growth, C where / food / stored, D when / plants / removed / earth, E type of farm; Questions 12–13 – negative aspects / organic farming; options – A Consumers complain / cost, B make people ill, C Farm workers / specially trained, D too much / technological expertise, E not possible / some countries)

❻ Tell students to run their eyes quickly over the passage again to find synonyms of the words they underlined, then read those sections carefully to find answers. To encourage scanning techniques, give students a strict time limit of four minutes.

Answers
8 B (from paragraph B: *Techniques such as crop rotation …*)
9 E (from paragraph B: *… compared to the amount of carbon dioxide …*)
10 B (from paragraph D: *… the amount of sunlight and rain crops have received …*)
11 D (from paragraph D: *… how long ago it was dug up.*)
12 B (from paragraph E: *… the closer a plant is to its natural state, the more likely it is that it will poison you.*)
13 E (from paragraph G: *… in rural Africa, it is a disaster.*)

Point out that for Questions 10–11, the answers are reflected in paragraph D and are cued by the sentence: *the health value of different foods will vary for a number of reasons*: B – *the amount of sunlight*; D – *how long ago it was dug up*. For Questions 12–13, the answer to B is reflected in paragraph E: *Toasting bread creates carcinogens; the closer a plant is to its natural state, the more likely it is that it will poison you.* The answer to E is reflected in paragraph G: *in rural Africa it is a disaster. Here, land tends to be so starved and crop yields so low that there simply is not enough organic matter to put back into the soil.*

❼ Encourage students to give reasons for their answers. You can develop this pair-work exercise into a whole-class discussion.

Listening   Section 2

❶ ***As a warmer*** Ask students to imagine they are going to talk to some people studying to become nurses in a hospital. Ask them to work in groups and brainstorm: ways in which a nurse's job might be stressful or unhealthy; advice they would give them about how to have a healthy lifestyle.

To help students get started with the exercise in the book, elicit some possible questions, e.g. *When did you last make a salad for yourself? What's your favourite dish? How often do you cook at home?*

Alternative treatment With weaker classes, ask students to work in pairs and think of a number of questions for each photo. They then change partners and take turns to ask and answer questions.

Extension idea To give students practice in speaking at length (useful for Speaking Part 2), when they finish this activity, ask them to change partners and summarise the information they learned from their previous partner. Tell them that they should each speak for a minute or two. The other student should just listen without interrupting.

2 Prepare students for the task before listening.

- Tell them that the words they hear when they listen will not be the same as the words used in the questions.

- Tell students to underline the key ideas in the questions.

> **Suggested answers**
> **1** why / fail / balanced diet   **2** staff / keep fit by
> **3** which benefit / most important   **4** what advice /
> health and safety   **5** hygiene / asks / nurses

- Elicit what is meant by *fail*, *balanced diet* and *hygiene*.

- Ask students how they would express the key ideas in the questions using their own words (this is a way of predicting how the ideas will be expressed when they listen).

3 🎧 You should play the recording once only as in the exam. Then ask students to work in pairs and compare answers. Play the recording again for them to check.

> **Answers**
> **1** B (*it's often too easy to grab something quick, because you're tired or busy*)
> **2** C (*it may just be a question of doing things differently*)
> **3** A (*you'll find that you don't lie awake at night*)
> **4** C (*you shouldn't work for more than three hours without a break*)
> **5** C (*don't leave even a small amount of rubbish around*)

Remind students that in the real test, they have to transfer their answers onto an answer sheet at the end. Therefore, it is important that they mark their answers clearly on the question paper so they can read them later.

4 As students do the exercise, clarify terms they may be unsure of, such as *south-west* and explain that they are not expected to know which way round they are standing with references to *right* or *left* – this is always explained on the recording. Elicit any other words or phrases they know related to position or location. Tell students to always check to see if the compass points (north, south, east, west) are on the map. If they are, the speaker may refer to them.

5 🎧 The aim of map-labelling tasks is to test students' ability to listen for detail and to follow directions and find locations.

> **Answers**
> **6** C   **7** B   **8** H   **9** E   **10** A

Vocabulary
Word formation

1 *As a warmer* With books closed, tell students they are going to work on word formation.

- Write examples on the board: *happy – happiness – happily – unhappy – unhappiness – unhappily*.

- Ask which words are adjectives, which are nouns and which are adverbs.

- Tell students to form small groups and give three minutes for them to think of as many words as they can form from:

  – *care* (*Possible answers*: careful, careless, carefully, carelessly, caring, uncaring, carer)

  – *success* (*Possible answers*: succeed, successful, successfully, unsuccessful, unsuccessfully)

  – *safe* (*Possible answers*: unsafe, safely, unsafely, safety)

  – *health* (see answers below)

- The group which thinks of the most words is the winner.

Refer students to the tables on word formation in the Language reference on page 100. Point out that these are only general indications, but that any particular word may change slightly differently. Also, since students must spell words correctly for answers in the IELTS test to be marked correct, it is useful to go through the spelling rules with them, and elicit from them their own examples for each rule.

> **Answers**
> **2** healthily   **3** unhealthy   **4** healthy
> **5** healthier   **6** healthiest

2

> **Answers**
> **2** healthily   **3** (un)healthy; healthier; healthiest

3

> **Answers**
> **2** -ly   **3** -ful; -y; -less; -able   **4** in-; ir-; un-

4 Remind students of the importance of correct spelling in the exam.

> **Answers**
> **2** ~~harmy~~ harmful   **3** ~~unconvenient~~ inconvenient
> **4** ~~usefull~~ useful   **5** ~~slightly~~ slight
> **6** ~~wealth~~ wealthy   **7** ~~easy~~ easily
> **8** ~~dramaticaly~~ dramatically

Speaking   Part 2

❶ *As a warmer* Ask students:

- in what situations they may have to speak for one or two minutes or more in real life (e.g. giving a speech at a wedding, giving a presentation in class).

- how they feel when they have to speak like this and what can make it difficult.

- if they have ever had to do this in English.

Ask students to work in pairs and look at the Exam information and prompt card.

- Give them two or three minutes to discuss and make notes about what they could talk about to answer the questions.

- Tell students to change partners and take turns to give their talks.

Extension idea Ask students to work in pairs and discuss:

- how helpful their notes were when giving the talk.

- how they could make their notes more useful.

❷ Tell students that they will listen to a candidate doing the same task. This model will give them ideas about how they can do these short talks and the sort of things they can say.

Answer
She talks about the place in photo C.

Note This is a good moment to do the Pronunciation section on intonation on page 23 which is based on Eva's talk.

❸

Answers
1 market   2 fresh   3 home   4 station   5 stalls
6 fish   7 lady   8 Sociable

❹ Tell students that it is important to use phrases like the ones in this exercise because it helps the examiner to follow what they are saying.

Answers
1 talk about   2 going to   3 tell you
4 what's it like   5 buy   6 mentioned   7 in all

Mention that the examiner may ask them a very simple question at the end of their talk and they only need to say 'yes' or 'no' in reply.

Extension idea Ask students to think of other phrases they could add to the lists.

❺ Tell students they only have a minute to make some notes, so they shouldn't write full sentences.

Extension idea Ask students to show their notes to their partners. Ask students which notes look easy to follow, and which will give them enough to say for up to two minutes.

❻ If you did the extension idea in Exercise 5, ask students to change partners to do this exercise. Tell students to keep talking till you say 'thank you'; look at your watch and give them two minutes.

Extension idea Before students give their talks, write this checklist on the board.

Did he/she …

… *start answering the points on the prompt card straight away?*

… *use a phrase to start the talk?*

… *use phrases to introduce new points?*

… *use a phrase to end the talk?*

… *deal with all the points on the prompt card?*

… *use his/her notes?*

… *keep speaking for the time allowed?*

Then, discuss the points in the checklist.

- Ask: *Why are they good things to do? Is there anything you would add to the checklist?*

- Tell the student who is listening to tick the points covered on the checklist. When their partner has finished speaking they should give feedback based on the checklist.

- Round up useful feedback from the whole class.

- Ask students to change roles, so the student who was listening gives their talk and repeats the process.

- If you have time, ask students to change partners and each take turns to give their talks again. This gives them the chance to put the feedback into practice.

Pronunciation
Intonation 1

❶

Extension idea Tell students to work in small groups.

- Ask them to listen as you say: *Yesterday, I went to the hairdressers, the supermarket and the gym* (with a rising intonation on *yesterday, hairdressers* and *supermarket* and a falling intonation on *gym*).

- Ask them to repeat.

- Ask them to tell the people in their group:

  – three things they did yesterday

  – three things they bought the last time they went shopping

  – three things they are going to do next weekend. (You can write these on the board to remind them).

- While each student speaks, the others listen to check if the intonation is appropriate.

Alternative treatment You can make the extension exercise above into a memory game, where each student adds something to what the previous student has said.

- 1st student: *Yesterday, I went to the cinema.*
- 2nd student: *Yesterday, I went to the cinema and a football match.*
- 3rd student: *Yesterday, I went to the cinema, a football match and university.*
- 1st student: *Yesterday, I went to the cinema, a football match, university and a music shop.*

The game continues until students cannot remember the list. While doing it, you should monitor for appropriate intonation, which is really the point of the game.

❷ Students can discuss the answers in pairs.

❸ 🎧

> **Answers**
> 1 … we're students, so we can't afford to eat in restaurants very often.
> 2 I really like going to the local market …
> 3 … everything you get there's fantastic – it's so fresh.
> 4 … it's a pedestrian street … you know, there are no cars …
> 5 There's a large number of stalls that sell food – and some shops too …
> 6 I've got a favourite stall, it's run by a little old lady …
> 7 As I've mentioned, I like it because the food tastes good but also it's a very sociable place.
> 8 All in all, I like it because it's a great place to go … it's a colourful experience.

❹ If necessary, play the recorded sentences again for students to imitate.

Writing   Task 2

❶ *As a warmer* Write the following sentences on the board:

- *I always eat my meals at the same times.*
- *I think a lot about the food I'm going to eat.*
- *I decide what food I eat.*

Tell students to work in small groups and tell each other how true each of the sentences is for them. Tell them to give reasons and examples with their answers.

Tell students that in this unit, they are focusing on IELTS Writing tasks where there are two questions to discuss. When students read the task, tell them to underline the things they must deal with while they're reading (e.g. *how their food has been produced*). Tell them they should always do this with Writing tasks, as they will lose marks if they don't answer the question exactly.

Note: students will not score above Band 5 for Task Response (content) if they only answer one of the questions; and if they misunderstand the topic (write a tangential response) they will score Band 4 or below for this criterion. (Losing marks in this way for content can also affect marks for the other criteria. Vocabulary, for example, is rated according to its relevance to the prompt.)

> **Answers**
> 2 F (There are two parts: whether the statement is true or not, and what influences people.)
> 3 F (Also need to discuss what influences people.)
> 4 T
> 5 F (The rubric only asks students to 'include any relevant examples from your own knowledge or experience'. If students don't have relevant examples, they can ignore this instruction.)

❷ Tell students that although they are talking in general, they can also include ideas from their personal experience while discussing these questions.

Alternative treatment Ask students to work in pairs, read the essay, and decide which ideas in the answer they agree with.

❸ Ask students to explain why each option is correct or incorrect. Encourage them to record useful phrases and expressions in their notebooks.

> **Answers**
> 1 Over time   2 As a result   3 In particular
> 4 also   5 On the other hand   6 In addition
> 7 Another   8 In fact   9 In conclusion   10 Although

Notes:

1 *Nowadays* is grammatically incorrect because it is used with the present simple. *Over time* refers to the recent past as well as the present, so the present perfect tense is used.

2 *As a result* and *therefore* link a cause with its effect or consequence; *therefore* is used more often when what comes afterwards can be proved (e.g. *I'm allergic to wheat and therefore I can't eat bread.*)

3 *In particular* is a linking phrase; *Especially* is an adverb.

4 *Also* and *as well* mean the same as *too* but they come in different positions in the sentence or clause. *Also* usually goes before the verb, so it is in the right position here. *As well* usually goes at the end of the clause (*worry about … as well*).

5 *On the other hand* is a linker that introduces an alternative argument; *on (the) one hand* introduces a first argument and is followed by a contrast later – often *on the other hand*.

6 *In addition* adds a further supporting argument to a previous point; *besides* also adds a point, but a more important, conclusive point than the original argument (e.g. *I don't think I'll drive to the IELTS test centre next week. Besides, I haven't got a car at the moment.*)

7 *Another* adds a point or argument to a list; *the other* usually adds a second point to a first, on the understanding that there are only two points in the list.

8 *So* introduces a logical consequence and could be used here. However, it has already been used in the previous sentence so this would be poor style. Plus the statement that follows is not necessarily a consequence. *In fact* is better because it means 'actually' and introduces more information.

9 *Concluding* is an adjective, not a linker.

10 *Even though* would be correct here, but *even* on its own is an adverb: *This journey is taking even longer than I expected.*

❹ Students can discuss this in their same small groups.

❺

> **Answers**
> 1 five paragraphs
> 2 a general statement about food production and attitudes towards this
> 3 in the introduction and conclusion
> 4 yes, in the fourth paragraph
> 5 first sentence in second and fourth paragraphs
> 6 students' own answers
> 7 students' own answers

❻ Students write their plans.

> **Suggested answers**
> Para. 1 - introduction: many ways to buy food / many attitudes
> Para. 2 - first influence: people shop to suit their lifestyle, e.g. single people, people with large families
> Para. 3 - people with time can think about how food is produced
> Para. 4 - second influence: where people live, e.g. fresh food easy to get in my country
> Para. 5 - conclusion: cost one factor / some value quality above it

Note: This would be a good moment to work on countable and uncountable nouns in the Key grammar section.

❼

> **Answers**
> 1 T 2 F 3 T 4 T 5 F

Notes:

1 If students copy the question or parts of the question into their answer (at any stage), the examiner will not include these words in the word count (or in the assessment of vocabulary) and this means that their answer may be short and they will lose marks.

2 Task 2 must always be written in essay form – if students use bullet points, they will lose marks for format and will not score above Band 5 for Task Response (content).

3 Evidence of planning is important for Coherence and Cohesion (organisation); a 'clear overall organisation' is required to achieve Band 6 or above.

4 Similarly, paragraphing is assessed at each Band level and students need to show that they can use paragraphs (even if they make mistakes) to score above Band 5.

5 The more accurate students' spelling is, the better. If spelling mistakes cause confusion for the reader, students may not achieve Band 6 for vocabulary.

❽ As before, while students read, encourage them to underline elements in the task they must deal with.

❾ ***Extension idea*** Ask students to write their plans in class. When they have done so, tell them to work in small groups and compare their plans and ideas. Round up ideas from the whole class.

Tell students that at this stage in the course, it's more important to get practice in answering the question well, rather than in answering in 40 minutes. It is probably a good idea, though, to ask them to do the writing task for homework.

❿

Key grammar
Countable and uncountable nouns

❶

Answers
attitudes [C]; *food* [U]

❷

Answers
food products [C]; *ways* [C]; *people* [C]; *time* [U]; *money* [U]; *aspects* [C]; *importance* [U]; *fish* [U]; *issue* [C]; *consumers* [C]; *factors* [C]; *interest* [U]

❸

Answers

countable nouns	uncountable nouns	countable or uncountable nouns
a (wide) range of	much	plenty of
many	a little	most
a/an	a great deal of	a lot of
(very) few	little	any
a few	a considerable amount of	some
a (large) number of		

❹

Answers
2 a few   **3** many   **4** a lot of   **5** much   **6** little
7 number   **8** a lot

Vocabulary and grammar review Unit 1

Answers

Vocabulary

❶ **2** affect   **3** trouble   **4** effect(s)   **5** problems   **6** effect

❷ **2** percentage   **3** percent   **4** percentage; percent
2 False (Australia, not the United States)   **3** True
4 False (second highest, not third)

Grammar

❸ **2** more quickly   **3** best   **4** most complicated
5 funnier   **6** bigger   **7** most successful   **8** safer

Vocabulary and grammar review Unit 2

Answers

Vocabulary

❶ **2** harmful   **3** enjoyment   **4** totally   **5** tasty
6 organically   **7** unhealthy   **8** criticise/criticize

❷ **2** activity/action   **3** danger   **4** fitness   **5** happiness
6 independence   **7** toxin/toxicity   **8** nutrition
9 reliance/reliability   **10** accuracy

Grammar

❸ 2 information   3 A balanced diet   4 pollution
5 knowledge   6 fast-food shops   7 a very stressful
lifestyle   8 research

❹ 2 a   3 little   4 much   5 amount of   6 plenty of
7 few   8 deal of

Unit 2 photocopiable activity: The food and culture forum

Time: 40 minutes

Objectives

- To practise giving one-minute talks and extended responses to questions about food and diet
- To practise using discourse markers to structure a talk
- To practise making notes before speaking
- To revise word formation

Before class

You will need one photocopy of the activity page on page 24 for each student.

In class

❶ *As a warmer* Ask students: *What was your last meal? Did you cook it yourself? Was it traditional or fast food? Do you think it was healthy?*

Tell students to skim the internet forum to find out which situation is most similar to their own country. Give a time limit of two minutes for this. Round up answers with the whole class.

If you have students from South Korea or Italy, ask them: *Do you agree with what writers say about food in your country?*

❷ Students work alone to complete exercises 2 and 3.

❸ Check answers with the whole class.

> **2**   **1** established   **2** tasty   **3** critical   **4** organically
> **5** original   **6** importance
>
> **3**   **1** So, let me tell you; as I've mentioned
> **2** I really like   **3** Like most people; all in all

❹ Put students in groups of three or four. Students work alone to prepare a one-minute talk for their group about eating habits in their own country. Give them two or three minutes to make notes about what they could talk about on this topic. They should try to include some of the phrases and vocabulary from exercises 2 and 3. During the preparation time,

students should also read through the follow-up questions and three more of their own, for example:

– *How do you think eating habits will change in your country over the next 50 years?*

– *Do you think schoolchildren should be taught how to cook traditional meals?*

- Each student delivers their talk to the group. At the end of the talk, the other members take turns to ask the follow-up questions, leading to a discussion of around five minutes for each group member. Encourage students to give full responses to the questions, giving reasons and extra details where possible.

- While students are doing the task, monitor for the correct use of discourse markers, vocabulary and intonation. Round up with the whole class when all the groups have finished. It's a good idea to start your feedback with positive comments about the talks.

Extension idea Students use their ideas from the forum to draw up a paragraph plan for the Writing task below. They then write up the essay, either in a subsequent class or for homework.

> **In an increasingly modernised and globalised world, it is inevitable that traditional cooking will be replaced by fast food and international dishes.**
>
> To what extent do you agree or disagree?
>
> Give reasons for your answer and include any relevant examples from your own knowledge or experience.
>
> Write at least 250 words.

The food and culture forum

❶ Skim the internet forum about food and culture below. Are the situations in the three countries similar or different from yours?

❷ Complete the gaps using the correct form of these words.

> critic   establish   important   organic   taste   origin

❸ Look at the underlined phrases. Which are used for … ?

1   starting points
2   introducing points
3   ending points

Hi, everybody! Welcome to the Food Culture Forum. This is a space where you can share and discuss ideas about food and cooking in different countries. This week's discussion is:
How are cooking and eating habits changing in today's globalised world?

Do you have any views or experiences you'd like to share?
Just add your posts here …

Username: Sun_Hee
Location: Seoul, South Korea
Date: March 25, 18.35

It's interesting to think about this question in relation to South Korea, where I live. <u>So, let me tell you</u> the basic facts. I would say that there are two main trends in Korean eating habits nowadays. Many people follow a traditional diet, so they often eat rice for every meal, along with vegetable and meat dishes, or soup. I would say that in general, older people tend to prefer ¹ well-................................ patterns of eating, for example having boiled rice for breakfast. However, <u>as I've mentioned</u>, there are two main trends, because the younger generation often have a more international-style breakfast of cereal or toast, partly because they're quicker to prepare when time is short, as well as being ² .... !

Username: Martin345
Location: Manchester, UK
Date: March 26, 10.10

I'm very happy to give a view from the UK. First of all, I wanted to say that I realise that many people from other countries who visit the UK tend to ³ .... our food! However, I don't think they're always justified. So much has changed here over the past 30 years or so. As well as being more interested in choosing ⁴ .... produced food, people are really curious about trying new dishes, so when you go to the supermarket, you'll find a huge range of styles on offer, from Spanish to Thai to Indian. The only problem is that sometimes we forget that our own traditional dishes are not bad at all. <u>That's why I really like</u> going out for fish and chips every few weeks!

Username: Andrea77
Location: Bologna, Italy
Date: March 26, 15.28

<u>Like most people here</u>, I'm very proud of our traditional cooking, which has had such an important effect not only in Italy but all around the world. You can eat pasta or pizza almost anywhere around the world, but of course I recommend that you come here and try the ⁵ .... version. I don't think you will be disappointed. We Italians are famous for our love of food and enjoying what you eat is a very important part of life here. However, global fast-food restaurants have also become popular here and I'm not against that. <u>All in all</u>, though, I do think it's important for us to remember the ⁶ .... of our traditional cooking and make sure that the next generation will maintain it.

---

❹ You are going to prepare a one-minute talk. Your teacher will explain what to do next.

Follow-up questions	
1 How healthy is your country's traditional diet?	4 .... ?
2 Which is more important in your country's traditional cooking: appearance or taste? Why?	5 .... ?
3 Are people in your country concerned about genetically engineered food products? Why (not)?	6 .... ?

Vocabulary extension

Unit 2

Abbreviations: n/pln = noun / plural noun; v = verb; adj = adjective; adv = adverb; p = phrase; T/I = transitive/intransitive; C/U = countable/uncountable

allergic (to) *adj* If you are allergic to a substance such as a food, it can make you ill.

battery farming / chickens *n* [C] Battery farming is the practice of keeping a large number of chickens in a very small space to produce meat and eggs cheaply. Battery chickens are chickens that are kept in this way.

be good for your health *p* If something is good for your health, it makes you more healthy.

brand *n* [C] a product that is made by a particular company

deliver goods *p* to take goods to people's houses or to the place they need to go

examine / look at the contents *p* to look at what is inside a container

fatty food *n* [C] food that contains a lot of fat

follow a recipe *vp* to use a list of instructions to prepare and cook a particular dish

food allergy *n* [C] If you have a food allergy, that food makes you ill.

food hall *n* [C] a department of a large store where food is sold

food preparation *n* [U] the act of preparing food to be eaten

fresh produce *n* [U] food that has not been frozen, put in cans, etc.

get a good deal *p* to manage to buy something for a price that is not very expensive

go on a diet *p* to eat less in order to become thinner

home cooking *n* [U] food that has been prepared and cooked at home

ingredients *pln* [C] the foods that are used to make a particular dish

main meal of the day *n* [C] the meal at which you eat the most food

mass production *n* [U] the process of producing very large numbers of goods by using machines in factories

on offer *p* If an item in a shop is on offer, it is available to buy at a cheaper price than usual.

order a meal *p* to tell a waiter what you want to eat in a restaurant

on sale *p* If something is on sale, it is available to buy in a shop.

on the menu *p* If a type of food or drink is on the menu, it is available buy in a restaurant or café.

on the shelves *p* If a shop has a product on the shelves, that product is available to buy there.

ready-made meals *pln* [C] meals that have been prepared and cooked before you buy them, so you only need to heat them

retailer *n* [C] someone who sells products to the public

staple *adj* A staple food is a basic and very important food such as rice, pasta or potatoes.

supply and demand *n* [U] the idea that the price of goods and services depends on how much of something is being sold and how many people want to buy it

two for the price of one *p* If a product is available to buy at two for the price of one, you can have two of them for the price usually charged for one.

vegetarian *n* [C] someone who does not eat meat or fish

value for money *n* [U] If you get value for money, the thing you buy is worth what you paid for it.

❶ **Complete the paragraph by writing one word/phrase from the box in each gap. There are three extra words/phrases you do not need to use.**

~~world~~	affects	although	as a result	effects	in fact	on the other hand
especially	percent	percentage	problem	so	therefore	trouble

We may think that different parts of the **(0)** ......*world*...... are becoming more and more similar, but culture shock is still a very common **(1)** .... for people who travel to another country. It **(2)** .... most travellers by making them anxious, homesick or uncomfortable in the new culture. **(3)** .... most people eventually grow accustomed to the new country, the **(4)** .... of culture shock can last for years.

It is likely that a lower **(5)** .... of tourists suffer from culture shock than people going to work or study in a new country. Tourists tend to spend time with other tourists and stay in international hotels. **(6)** ...., they do not live with the local population or have to cope with the culture.

Culture shock is **(7)** .... strong for people going to work abroad. On the one hand, they have to deal with a difficult new working environment and **(8)** .... they do not get the support which students or other overseas visitors receive. **(9)** ...., nearly 30 **(10)** .... of overseas workers and their families find culture shock so hard to cope with that they return home early.

❷ **Complete the text by writing the words in brackets in the correct form.**

Many aspects of city life, such as pollution, may be **(0)** ....*harmful*.... (harm) to our health and general well-being and most people find living and working in big cities **(1)** .... (stress). They are **(2)** .... (general) in such a hurry that they do not eat well. Also, their exercise routine tends to be **(3)** .... (regular) and there may be many days or weeks when they take no exercise at all.

However, studies show that it is extremely important to be **(4)** .... (care) about what you eat. A **(5)** .... (health) diet should include plenty of fresh fruit and vegetables. On the other hand, you can put on weight **(6)** .... (ease) if you eat well but do not take exercise, so it is important to take a **(7)** .... (reason) amount of exercise every day to stay fit. Unfortunately, our routines often make it **(8)** .... (convenient) or difficult to find time for regular exercise. When people start to take exercise, their feeling of well-being often increases **(9)** .... (dramatic) and they also benefit from an increased level of **(10)** .... (fit).

❸ Complete the sentences with the correct form of the adjective or adverb in brackets.

0   The film was ..*more interesting*.. (interesting) than I expected.

1   If you study in the country where the language is spoken, you will learn to speak it
    .... (well) than if you stay at home.

2   My diet has improved because I eat .... (little) meat than I did in the past.

3   In my experience, rich people are not always .... (happy) than poor people.

4   Taking exercise outdoors is .... (enjoyable) than going to a gym.

5   They gave the prize to Saleem because he was the student in the class who had worked the
    .... (hard).

6   People won't understand you unless you speak .... (clearly) than you do now.

7   The distance from London to Bangkok is .... (far) than the distance to Moscow.

8   Pollution in my country is growing .... (bad), because nowadays there is more
    traffic and more industry.

9   In Australia, January is often the .... (hot) month of the year.

10 Brisbane had the second .... (high) rainfall in its history this year.

❹ Choose the best alternative (A, B, or C) for each of these sentences.

0   There are not as ....**A**........ overseas students at the university this year as last year.
    A many   **B** much   **C** little

1   This leaflet does not give very .... information about the city.
    A many   **B** much   **C** little

2   In my view, there is a .... of ways in which the situation could be improved.
    A great deal of   **B** large amount   **C** large number

3   Most foreigners have difficulty understanding our culture because .... of them manage to
    learn the language.
    A few   **B** little   **C** a few

4   There are .... opportunities to study abroad when you are a student.
    A a great deal of   **B** plenty of   **C** a large amount of

5   The schools have poor exam results because the government spends .... money on schools.
    A any   **B** few   **C** little

❺ Complete these sentences by writing a preposition (by, for, with, to, etc.) in each gap.

0   Culture shock is defined ....*as*.......... the physical and emotional discomfort a person
    experiences when entering a culture different from their own.

1   Living abroad can give rise .... feelings of homesickness.

2   From my point .... view, people can learn a lot from going to live somewhere new.

3   After spending several months in the city, I became accustomed .... the way of life.

4   Attitudes .... organic food are changing.

5   Preparing food can take up a lot of time. .... the other hand, it can be enjoyable.

Unit 3 Getting the message across

Unit objectives

- **Listening Section 3:** how to 'pick from a list'; introduction to matching and short-answer question tasks
- **Reading Section 3:** introduction to Yes / No / Not Given and summary-completion tasks; multiple choice
- **Vocabulary:** words and phrases connected with education: *teach, learn* and *study, find out* and *know*; vocabulary describing trends and changes
- **Speaking Part 2:** telling a story during the long turn – organising the story; organising vocabulary
- **Pronunciation:** consonant sounds – /ʃ/ and /dʒ/, /l/ and /r/, /v/ and /w/
- **Key grammar:** tenses – past simple, present perfect and present perfect continuous
- **Writing Task 1:** describing trends in a line graph and a table; organising and planning your answer; prepositions for describing trends

Starting off

❶ *As a warmer* With books closed, write on the board: *in class, alone with a teacher, studying alone.* Tell students to work in small groups and discuss the following questions.

- What things can you learn best in each situation?
- Which is the most enjoyable way of studying?

Then ask them to open their books and do the exercise.

> **Answers**
> 1 D   2 C   3 A   4 B

❷ Encourage students to expand their answers: they should answer the second question by talking about their personal experience, and the third by giving reasons and examples.

> **Suggested answer**
> 1 All the situations are study-related.

Listening   Section 3

❶ *As a warmer* There are many countries where universities do not have a tutorial system, so this may be an unfamiliar concept to some of your students. Focus on photo B. Ask students:

- *What (do you think) happens in university tutorials?* (*Answer*: the tutor gives feedback to individual students about their work, advice on how and what to study, and sets assignments. He/she also assesses the students' work and helps them with it.)

- *What do you think are the advantages of a tutorial system at college or university?*

- Students then do the matching exercise.

> **Answers**
> 2 b   3 a   4 g   5 c   6 i   7 e   8 h   9 f

Extension idea To activate the vocabulary, ask students to work in groups and each choose a word or phrase from 1–9. They should then talk about the word or phrase in relation to their own learning experiences.

❷ Refer students to the Exam overview on page 7 and the features of Section 3 of the Listening test. In this part, they hear a conversation between two or more speakers. Point out that unlike Sections 1 and 2, the third and fourth Sections of the Listening test are based on educational or study situations. Section 3 in particular often involves vocabulary related to these contexts.

- Tell students that this is like an extended multiple-choice question. As there is more than one answer, though, it is particularly important to read the questions carefully so that they know what to listen for. They should also note how many marks they get. The rubric *Questions 1–2* means that each correct answer scores one mark, as there is one mark per question in the Listening test.

> **Suggested answers**
> **1–2** TWO activities / students do / Amanda's assignment
> **3–4** TWO features / Amanda check / chooses the extract)

Extension idea In order to focus students on the five options, tell them to read Questions 1–2 and then ask:

- *What is the difference between options A and B?* (*Answer*: The function words are different. A is about someone's own speech, while B is about someone else's speech.)

- *What is the difference between options D and E?* (*Answer*: The verbs are different. D involves speaking, while E involves memory.)

- *Why is C different from the others?* (*Answer*: Option C stands out because it is about a book.)

Then ask students to read Questions 3–4 and to decide how the options are different. (*Suggested answers*: A is the only option that doesn't describe something about the content of the extract; C and D are both about 'how many'; B is about structure and E is about content.)

❸ 🎧 Play this part once only, as in the exam. Students then work in pairs to compare answers. Play it a second time so they can check their answers.

- Point out that the 'wrong' options are often mentioned in the recording, so students should avoid simply matching words they hear to words on the question paper without listening to the whole utterance. For example, the word *record* in option B is mentioned in *You mean, get them to record themselves*. If students listen on, however, they will realise that they are not going to record 'other students' speech' but their own.

> **Answers**
> **1–2** A (*... record themselves ... then listen back and see where their weaknesses lie ...*) and D (*... look up one of my lectures ... and find a suitable extract ...*)
> **3–4** B (*a clear, well-structured passage*) and E (*some obvious main points*)

❹ Before looking at these questions, ask students to look at Questions 5–8 and elicit what they have to do (*Answer*: match the comments to the lectures).

- Before they start, advise students to use the numbered items – in this case the lectures – to guide their listening. They will hear these stated on the recording in question order. When they hear the first of these (*History of English*) it should alert them to the fact that the answer to this question is coming.

> **Answers**
> **1** lecture titles
> **2** A content / repetitive; B long time / write; C shorter; D well structured; E content / relevant; F topic / popular
> There are two extra options
> **3** just the letters (A, B, C, etc.)

❺ Short-answer questions test students' ability to pick out a particular detail or piece of information. The answers are usually nouns, and often concrete details. Students underline the key ideas.

> **Suggested answer**
> TWO pieces of equipment

❻ 🎧 Ask students to listen once and compare answers in pairs.

- Play the recording again for students to check answers.

- For Questions 5–8, you can elicit what words and phrases in the recording gave students the answers.

> **Answers**
> **5** D (*clearly sequenced and presented*)
> **6** F (*went down well / I really liked that one*)
> **7** E (*topic's certainly more closely linked*)
> **8** C (*mini-lectures / wouldn't have to spend too much time*)

Alternative treatment for Questions 9–10 students often hear the correct answer, but lose marks because they spell it wrongly. Ask students how they spelled the answers; write the different spellings on the board and ask which is correct.

> **Answers**
> **9** mobile phone(s) **10** digital recorder(s)

Extension idea Ask students to work in small groups. They tell each other about an assignment or project they have worked on recently, either in their studies or their work.

Reading   Section 3

❶ *As a warmer* With books closed, write on the board:

- *At what age do children learn ...?*
  ... to talk
  ... to read and write

- *When they first learn to talk, what sort of things do they say?*

Ask students to work in small groups and discuss the questions. If teaching a multinational class, try to form groups with mixed nationalities for more contrast. Get feedback from the whole class, then ask students to open their books and discuss the questions.

Extension idea 1 Elicit what problems there are in understanding baby language. (*Suggested answer*: Because it lacks grammar, it's ambiguous or difficult to know exactly what the baby wants to say.)

Extension idea 2 Ask students why language teachers are so interested in how babies learn to talk. (*Suggested answer*: Because young children learn their mother tongue so effectively, perfectly and apparently effortlessly, it might indicate methods for learning second or foreign languages.)

② Point out that the Section 3 Reading text is usually the most difficult; it often contains research-based arguments and a range of views, like the one here.

- Quickly elicit the key stages of research: hypothesis – method – experiment – results – findings – conclusions.

- Before doing this exercise, and in order to encourage good exam technique, elicit from the class: *What are the first things you should do before you start a reading section?* (*Suggested answer*: Look at the title and the subheading, glance through the passage to see how long it is, look quickly to see what tasks you will have to do.)

Suggested answer
Something about how babies learn to talk and the stages they go through.

③ To encourage skimming, give students three minutes to read the whole passage quickly. Be strict about keeping to the time you set.

Suggested answer
When their brains are ready.

④ Yes / No / Not Given questions test students' ability to scan for specific information and then to read the relevant part of the passage in detail to fully understand the writer's ideas or opinions. Point out the following to students.

- These questions are similar to True / False / Not Given, but whereas those questions deal with facts and information, Yes / No / Not Given deals with the writer's opinions and claims. Explain what a 'claim' is. (*Answer*: It's something that the writer believes to be true, but which cannot be proved

and other people might not believe.). Students do not need to worry too much about this distinction, but should expect to see the words *claim* or *opinion* in the rubric.

- As in True / False / Not Given questions, unless the question specifically contradicts an idea or opinion in the passage (NO), the answer is NOT GIVEN.

- Some of the words or phrases in the question will be the same or similar to words in the passage. Students should scan the passage to find similar words and then read carefully around them to decide their answer. Diagrams have been included with Question 1 to help students with this.

Answer
1 YES

⑤ Ask students to work in pairs and compare what they have underlined in each question before reading.

Suggested answers
2 Behaviourists / learn to speak / copying
3 Children / more conversations / adults / other children
4 Scientists / work out / one-word sentences

Give students three minutes to locate and underline where Questions 2–4 are answered in the passage. (*Suggested answers*: 2 *Behaviourism, the scientific approach that dominated American cognitive science …* 3 *However, this copycat theory … aren't as conversational as adults.* 4 *What is hard for them to do …*) Students shouldn't read carefully to answer the questions at this stage.

Answers
2 YES   **3** NOT GIVEN   **4** NO

⑥ This task usually tests students' understanding of ideas. They need to use the title to scan for the correct part of the passage and then read in detail.

- Give students a minute to do this and then compare answers in pairs. They should match *two main theories* with *two reasonable possibilities* in the fourth paragraph.

- Tell students to look at Question 5 and decide what type of word or phrase is missing (*Answer*: a noun – something the brain needs).

- Students then look at the underlined words around Question 5 and quickly read the part of the passage they have chosen for words that are the same or mean the same (*One – The first of these; young child's – one-year-olds; master language – speak multi-word sentences or use word endings and function words*).

- Students read around these sections carefully and underline the word(s) which will give the answer to Question 5. Ask: *How do the words 'until' and 'before' help you match the answer in the passage to option C?*

> **Answer**
> The words in the fourth and fifth sentences of paragraph 4 suggest that some time has to pass before children can do these things.

7 Tell students to work on Questions 6–9 using the same techniques used to answer Question 5. Ask them, when they've finished, to read the whole summary again to check that it reads grammatically and makes sense. They should also check that it reflects the ideas they have understood from the passage.

Alternative treatment Students work in pairs. Ask them to look at the gapped summary and the list of words and phrases without reading the passage, to see which will fit in each gap. They should have several possibilities for each. Ask them to predict which answer will be correct in each case. They then read the passage to check if their predictions are correct.

> **Answers**
> **6** B **7** A **8** F **9** E

8 Multiple-choice questions test students' ability to skim or scan to find the relevant section of the passage and then to read in detail and discriminate between the correct answer and distracting information.

Students should use the stem of the multiple-choice question (e.g. in Question 10, *What is the writer's main purpose in the sixth paragraph?*) to help them find the part of the passage which answers the questions, before looking at options A–D. It can be confusing to look at the options first and then read the text to find the correct answer. In most cases, better results are obtained by understanding the passage first and then finding the option which corresponds.

Alternative treatment Ask students to look at each question, but not the options. Ask them to find the answers in the passage and then work in pairs and explain them in their own words. Once they have finished, they then work together to choose correctly from options A–D.

> **Answers**
> **1 Suggested underlining**
> **10** writer's purpose
> **11** Snedeker / Geren, Shafto / study / children
> **12** aspect / adopted / language development / differed / US-born
> **13** what / Harvard finding show

> **14** critical period
> **2 10** A (*All of these factors make them an ideal population in which to test these competing hypotheses about how language is learned.*)
> **11** C (*These children began learning English at an older age than U.S. natives and had more mature brains with which to tackle the task.*)
> **12** C (*The adoptees then went through the same stages as typical American-born children, albeit at a faster clip.*)
> **13** B (*Learning how to chat like an adult is a gradual process.*)
> **14** D (*Researchers have long suspected there is a 'critical period' for language development, after which it cannot proceed with full success to fluency.*)

9 *Extension idea* To give students practice speaking at length, when they have finished discussing these questions, ask them to change groups and present the opinions and conclusions expressed in their original groups. The other students should listen and say which ideas they agree with.

Speaking Part 2

1 *As a warmer*

- With books closed, ask students to think of a time when they had difficulty communicating in a foreign language. Give them a couple of minutes to think.

- Then tell them to work in small groups and take turns to tell each other their stories.

- Still with books closed, elicit what Speaking Part 2 consists of. (*Suggested answer*: They are given a prompt card with a topic and questions. They have a minute to prepare and take notes. They then have to speak for between one and two minutes. The examiner may ask one or two follow-up questions at the end.) Students then do the exercise in the book.

> **Answers**
> where you were: **1, 5**
> what happened: **4, 8**
> how well you communicated in the language: **6, 7**
> why you remember this situation or experience: **2, 3**

2 *Alternative treatment* Before they listen, ask students to predict what the experience might be about from the notes in Exercise 1. They then listen to check and make their own notes.

Extension idea Ask students to work in pairs and briefly re-tell Abi's story.

Note: This is a good moment to do the Pronunciation section on consonant sounds, which is based on Abi's talk.

❸ 🎧 Before students listen again, ask them how many of the phrases they can place. They then listen and place the rest.

Elicit what *eventually* and *as soon as* mean in this context. (*Answers: eventually* = in the end, especially after a long time or a lot of effort or problems; *as soon as* = at the same time or a very short time after)

introducing a stage in the story	giving reasons / explanations
A couple of years ago	This was because
Eventually	The reason why
So the next thing we did	
Before we went	
At the time	
As soon as	
However, one morning	

Extension idea 1 Ask students to work in pairs and remember how Abi used these phrases (i.e. what he actually said).

Extension idea 2 Ask students to add a phrase of their own to each column. When they have done this, round up ideas with the whole class and write them on the board.

If students have difficulty thinking of other phrases, try eliciting these by suggesting one word (*Suggested answers: Last … night/week/month; a few … days ago; When I was … 16 / living with my parents; In the … morning/afternoon; At …5 o'clock / supper time; In the … end*)

Note: This is a good moment to do the Pronunciation section on consonant sounds, and the Key grammar section on tenses, which are both based on Abi's talk.

❹ If students are stuck for ideas, tell them to look at the images and imagine themselves in one of the situations. Give them a minute to make notes.

❺ Before doing this exercise, tell students that they will give their talks in pairs and that the student who is listening will give feedback to their partner. Ask them

if they remember giving feedback in Unit 2 and what they had to check. Ask them to work in pairs and make a list of criteria. Round up with ideas from the whole class. (*Suggestions:* Did he/she answer all the points, keep going for more than a minute, introduce and round off the talk, use some of the signposting phrases in this section, use past tenses correctly, use his/her notes, sound interested in what he/she was saying, look at you while speaking?)

Alternative treatment You can adopt the following procedure for doing the talks:

- the first student gives their talk.
- the second student gives feedback to first student.
- you round up feedback with whole class.
- the second student gives their talk, taking into account feedback given earlier to other students.
- the first student gives feedback to second student.

❻ As in the exam, give students one minute for this.

❼ If your class needs, follow the same procedure as suggested for Exercise 5.

Pronunciation
Consonant sounds

Note: Sound production is one of the features of pronunciation that examiners take into consideration when they give a score for this criterion.

Tell students that there are two main areas:

- the general number of mistakes in English sounds;
- how much these mistakes affect communication.

In other words, the more errors there are and the greater the level of impact on the listener, the lower the Band score. (Examiners also consider other features of pronunciation and form an overall view of pronunciation, but sound production can have a significant impact on everything else.)

Different language-speakers have different problems with the consonant sounds of English. If your students don't have problems with the sounds featured in this section C /ʃ/ and /dʒ/, /l/ and /r/, /v/ and /w/), you should omit it, but tell your students why. Similarly, if it is only necessary to concentrate on some of the sounds, explain why.

❶ 🎧 Elicit from students, or tell them, what each of the words given as examples means (*answers: sheep* = a farm animal; *jeep* = a type of car; *climb* = use your legs to go up; *crime* = illegal activities; *vent* = a small opening which allows air to escape an enclosed space; *went* = past of go). Then ask students to listen and repeat, perhaps in pairs.

② 🎧 *Alternative treatment* Ask students to fill the gaps first, then check their answers by listening.

> **Answers**
> **2** reason   **3** lives   **4** just   **5** waiting   **6** she

③ *Extension idea* Ask one or two volunteers to read the paragraph aloud to the rest of the class. The other students give feedback on the consonant sounds the volunteers had problems with.

④ Ask students to look at the script.

Vocabulary
Teach, learn or *study*? *Find out* or *know*?

① *As a warmer* With books closed, write *learn, teach* and *study* on the board. Tell students to work alone and write one thing they have learned, one thing they have taught and one thing they have studied recently. Then they work in small groups and read out their answers. The other students in the group ask questions to find out more (e.g. *How did you learn it? Who did you teach it to? Why did you study that?*, etc.).

> **Answers**
> **2** found out   **3** learn   **5** Learning   **6** know

② To get students started, ask them to look at extract 1 and elicit why *known* is correct (*answer: know* is for knowledge you have had for some time, *find out* is for things you learn which are new). Point out that *learn* and *find out* can be interchangeable (e.g. *I was delighted when I learned / found out that we had won the football match*). In this case, the speaker is not actively 'learning' or 'finding out' but passively receiving information about something that they did not know beforehand.

③

> **Answers**
> **2** learn   **3** teach   **4** find out   **5** study

④ *Extension idea* Ask students to think of three or four extra questions. They then change partners and ask and answer their questions.

Key grammar
Tenses

① Tell students that they will often have to talk about something which happened to them in the past when they do Speaking Part 2, so it is important to use tenses referring to the past correctly.

> **Answers**
> **1** b   **2** a   **3** c

②

> **Answers**
> **a** 2   **b** 3   **c** 1

③

> **Answers**
> **4** went; hired; picked up; reached (past simple)
> **5** didn't know (past simple)
> **6** arrived (past simple)
> **7** have I learned (present perfect)

④ When students have finished the exercise, it is worth going through the explanation in the Language reference with them on page 103.

> **Answers**
> **1** d   **2** a   **3** b   **4** c   **5** a   **6** a   **7** b

⑤ Tell students to pay special attention to choosing the correct tense both when speaking and writing.

> **Answers**
> **2** visited   **3** have been   **4** has become
> **5** ate   **6** was

Writing   Task 1

① *As a warmer* With books closed, ask students (or write on the board so students can discuss in groups):

- *Which are the main foreign languages taught in schools in your country?*
- *Why do students choose to study those languages?*
- *How has the choice of languages changed in recent years?*
- *What languages do you think students will choose in the future?*

Alternative treatment Ask students to work in pairs and write their answer to the five questions. They then compare their answers with another pair. Encourage them to use their own words rather than lifting from the words in the task.

> **Suggested answers**
> **1** It shows how many 13-year-old students took French and Mandarin in a school in England between 2000 and the present.
> **2** They are opposites. Figures for French have gradually fallen. Figures for Mandarin have risen.
> **3** Significant similarities: the 2010 figure. Significant differences: 2000 and the trend to 2005.

4 French: the fall to 2005 / the rise to 2006 and the stable pattern to now.

Mandarin: the rise to 2005 / the dip in 2006 and the fluctuation to now.

5 Paragraph 1: introduction and summary of main trends.

Paragraph 2: summary of trends and differences/similarities.

Paragraph 3: overview of graph.

Extension idea Ask students to draw a graph showing trends for two subjects in a school in their country. They can invent the statistics. They then work in pairs and talk each other through the graphs they have drawn. Alternatively, they can give their graph to the other student, who then has to describe the information drawn by their partner.

❷ Elicit from the whole class why e is the first sentence (*Answer*: it says what the graph shows). Then elicit which is the final sentence and why; this will give students a framework to fit the other sentences into the correct order. (*Answer*: a – it gives an overview of all the information summarised.)

Answers
e, h, f, c, g, b, j, d, i, a

Complete answer
The graph shows how many 13-year-old students studied French and Mandarin between 2000 and the present day in a school in England. According to the data, Mandarin has increased in popularity during this time. On the other hand, the trend for French is the opposite. In 2000, the number of students who took French was 150, compared to just under 10 students who chose Mandarin. So there was a significant difference in numbers at this time. Over the next five years, the figure fell considerably for French, but rose dramatically for Mandarin and reached a peak at 75 students. Since 2005, the trends have not changed as much. French gained some popularity in 2006 but has remained fairly stable since then at about 90 students. In contrast, the number of students taking Mandarin dipped in 2006 and then fluctuated, before it returned to 75. Overall, it can be seen that more students have been choosing to study Mandarin, but French is still the most popular language option.

❸ Elicit why it is important to use more phrases than *went up* and *went down* (*Answer*: a variety of vocabulary is better style and shows students' range. Candidates are marked down for repeating the same words because their vocabulary resource

appears limited. Also, a range of words and phrases will improve their mark; it can make the difference between a Band 5 and a Band 6 score for this criterion.)

Answers
1 fell; dipped **2** reached a peak **3** has remained fairly stable **4** rose dramatically **5** fluctuated

❹ Tell students it is important that they become familiar with a variety of ways of presenting information, and with looking for trends and comparisons within the information. (Tables are common in Writing Task 1.)

Answers
The table provides some background information on the staff working in a global hotel chain. The information goes back to 1975 and covers languages spoken and qualifications, as well as previous work experience. **1** the percentage of staff who speak two or more languages **2** the percentage of staff who have previous work experience **3** the percentage of staff who have a language qualification

Extension idea Ask students to draw a line chart which shows the same information contained in the table. This may help students who are visually minded to understand it better (though you should tell them not to do this in the exam itself, as they won't have time).

❺

Answer		
1 5 percent	**2** 22 percent	**3** 2 percent
4 10 percent	**5** 23 percent	**6** 79 percent
7 78 percent	**8** 55 percent	

❻

Answers
a significant rise; slight fall; rose; rocketed; fluctuated; a peak; a sudden fall; went up and down

❼

Suggested answer
Languages have become more important than experience in the hotel industry since 1975, but far more staff can speak other languages than have qualifications.

With students, review why an overview is important. (*Answer*: students need to write an overview to achieve a high band score – it shows they can give a general view of what the information shows, not just a breakdown of the details.) Also review how an overview differs from an introduction. (*Answer*: an introduction says what the summary will be about, while an overview gives a general summary of the main or most important data in the charts.)

8 You should go through the Language reference on prepositions on page 102 with students before they attempt this exercise. Point out that there are rules for using prepositions to describe trends and that it is useful to learn them for doing Writing Task 1. Encourage students to refer to the Language reference section while they're doing the exercise.

> **Answers**
> **2** between **3** by **4** of **5** in **6** to **7** at

9

> **Answers**
> **2** increased ~~over~~ **from** **3** a rise ~~of~~ **in**
> **4** peaked ~~to~~ **at** **5** fell ~~on~~ **by** **6** decreased ~~until~~ **to**
> **7** ~~During the period of~~ **Between** 1986 **and** 1999
> **8** an increase ~~by~~ **of**

10 *Extension idea 1* When students have finished planning their answer, ask them to change partners and compare their ideas.

This writing task is probably best done for homework. Tell students they would have about 20 minutes for this in the exam, but that at this stage in the course, they should concentrate on producing a good answer, so if they take a little longer it doesn't matter.

> **Sample answer**
>
> The line graph shows the percentage of new graduates who found jobs as teachers of English and French in Ontario each year from 2001 to 2007.
>
> At the beginning of the period, teachers of both languages had approximately a 70% success rate in finding jobs, although French teachers were slightly less successful than English teachers. The following year, recruitment for both categories fell by approximately 15% to 55%.
>
> However, in 2003, teachers of French began to be more successful at finding employment than their English-teaching colleagues. Their recruitment rate rose to nearly 70%, where it stabilised, with minor variations, until 2007 when it rose again to just under 75%.
>
> On the other hand, the employment of new graduates as English teachers decreased sharply to 40% in 2003. During the following two years, the number acquiring jobs rose slightly to 44% in 2005 before falling to just over 25% in 2007.
>
> Overall, the graph shows new graduates in Ontario managed to find more jobs as French teachers than as English teachers in the same period.

Extension idea 2 Set a deadline for students to bring their answers to class. Ask them to work in pairs and to read each other's answers to check that:

- they have included an overview.
- they have varied the vocabulary they use.
- they have used the correct form of each verb.
- they have used prepositions correctly.

Ask them to correct any mistakes they find. Discuss anything they are not sure about with the whole class before they hand in their answers.

Unit 3 photocopiable activity: This is your academic life

Time: 25 minutes

> **Objectives**
> - to increase fluency when talking about student life
> - to practise the use of tenses

Before class

You will need to photocopy the activity page on page 36 and cut it up so that each group of students has one set of grey and one set of white cards.

In class

1 Tell students that they are going to do a speaking activity to practise the past simple, present perfect and present perfect continuous.

2 Ask them to work in groups of three or four and place the two sets of cards (grey and white) in two separate piles, face down, on the table.

3 First, write on the board: *Talk about a difficult exam you took.* Elicit phrases for introducing a stage in a story (e.g. *A couple of years ago*; *At the time*; *As soon as*; *eventually*). Then elicit phrases for giving reasons/ explanations (e.g. *the reason why*; *this was because*). Write these phrases on the board. Then talk about the subject in one minute, using some of the phrases.

4 Next, demonstrate a 'Grammar Check' card by writing the following sentence on the board: *I have been teach for 10 years.* Ask the class to say whether it is correct or not, and to give the correct version (*I have been teaching for 10 years*).

5 During the game, monitor the students' use of tenses and phrases for organising a story, noting down any typical errors. With a strong group, you may wish to ask students themselves to write down any errors they hear when their partners are speaking.

6 When all the groups have finished, write a selection of errors on the board and asking students to correct them. Go through each error with the class.

This is your academic life

Talk about a time when you worked successfully with another student.	Talk about a book which you have been reading for study purposes in recent months.	Talk about the first time you took an exam or test.	Describe a website which you have been using for your studies over the past few months.
Talk about a presentation you have given.	Describe your first day at high school or college.	Talk about a piece of writing you have been working on recently.	Talk about any lecture or lesson which you didn't enjoy.
Talk about any lesson or lecture which you enjoyed.	Were you a good student at primary school? Give examples.	Talk about a happy day you spent with school or college friends.	Describe a difficult assignment you have completed.
Talk about a school or college social event that you went to.	Do you prefer to express your ideas in writing or by speaking? Why?	Describe a stressful day you had at school or college.	Talk about a teacher who helped you a lot with your studies.

Since I was a child I've always loved finding out about new things. ✔	On my first day at high school, I have felt really nervous. ✘ On my first day at high school, I felt really nervous.
Our school canteen improved a lot after the students complained. ✔	When the day of the exam came, I have been terrified. ✘ When the day of the exam came, I was terrified.
I have been graduating from high school last year. ✘ I graduated from high school last year.	When I have been younger, I wasn't interested in reading. ✘ When I was younger, I wasn't interested in reading.
I was interested in mathematics since I was at school. ✘ I have been interested in mathematics since I was at school.	She was the best teacher I've ever had. ✔
He has been a good teacher because he was able to explain things. ✘ He was a good teacher because he was able to explain things.	I studied English since I was twelve. ✘ I have studied/have been studying English since I was twelve.
It was the most interesting lecture I ever been to. ✘ It was the most interesting lecture I've ever been to.	I have been meeting my best friend on the first day at school. ✘ I met my best friend on the first day at school.
Recently, I have become more interested in academic research. ✔	I've been studying at university for two years now. ✔
So far, I've never been giving a group presentation. ✘ So far, I've never given a group presentation.	I practised regularly over the past week. ✘ I've been practising regularly over the past week.

Vocabulary extension

Unit 3

Abbreviations: n/pln = noun / plural noun; v = verb; adj = adjective; adv = adverb; p = phrase;
T/I = transitive/intransitive; C/U = countable/uncountable

apply to an institution *p* to make an official request to go to a place such as a college or university

bibliography *n* [C] a list of books and articles on a particular subject

coursework *n* [U] work done by students as part of their course of study

course curriculum *n* [C] the subjects that are taught as part of a particular course of study

course materials *n* [C] books, equipment, etc. that are used in a course of study

department *n* [C] a part of an organisation such as a college or university where a particular subject is taught and studied

dissertation *n* [C] a long piece of writing done as part of a course of study

do research *p* to study a subject, especially to discover new information about it

faculty *n* [U] a department or a group of departments in a college or university

fellow students *pln* [C] people who are students at the same time as you are

future career *n* [C] Someone's future career is the series of jobs that they will have in their life.

gap year *n* [C] a year between leaving school and starting university which you usually spend travelling or working

get the right grades *p* to get the marks you need in an exam

get a good degree *p* to get a good mark in the qualification you take at the end of a university course

give up (a subject or course) *p* to stop doing (a subject or course) before you have completed it

lecture hall *n* [C] a large room with rows of seats where students sit to hear lectures

plagiarise *v* T to take someone else's work, ideas or words and use them as if they were your own

postgraduate *n* [C] a student who has one degree and now studies at a university for a more advanced degree

post-secondary education *n* [U] education that a student does after secondary school

quote (sources or references) *v* T to give a fact or example (from another document or writer) in order to support what you are saying

receive funding *p* to be given money for a particular purpose

sponsorship *n* [C] money that is given to support an event or activity

student union *n* [C] an organisation of students in a college or university which arranges social events and provides services to support students

syllabus *n* [C] a plan showing the subjects or books to be studied in a particular course

take (a course or subject) *v* T to study (a course or subject)

teaching staff *n* [U] the people who are employed to teach in an organisation

the education system *n* [C] all the organisations that are involved in providing education

tuition fees *pln* amounts of money that students must pay to be taught at a university or college

undergraduate *n* [C] a student who is studying for their first university degree qualification

university campus *n* [C] the buildings of a university and the land that surrounds them

university places *pln* The number of university places is the number of students that universities can take.

work to a deadline *vp* to have to finish a piece of work by a particular time or date

Unit 4 New media

Unit objectives

- **Reading Section 1**: practising skimming; True / False / Not Given; introduction to note-completion and short-answer questions
- **Listening Section 4**: introduction to summary completion and flow-chart completion
- **Vocabulary**: *cause*, *factor* and *reason*; Internet-related words and phrases
- **Speaking Parts 2 and 3**: preparing vocabulary for Part 2; using reasons and examples to extend Part 3 answers; expressing uncertainty and possibilities
- **Pronunciation**: introduction to chunking
- **Writing Task 2**: analysing the task; brainstorming ideas; work on opening paragraph; essay planning and structuring; *however, although, even though, on the other hand*
- **Key grammar**: articles

Starting off

❶ *As a warmer* With books closed, and in order to train students with brainstorming:

- ask them to work in small groups and make a list of as many different types of media as possible (e.g. television). Give two minutes for this. You can make this a competition – the group with the longest list is the winner.
- give one medium to each group (e.g. group 1 – radio, group 2 – newspapers, etc.). Tell the groups to think of as many different uses for their type of media as possible (e.g. radio – to listen to music). Give two minutes for this.
- Encourage students to give reasons for their answers when they do the task in the book.

Reading Section 1

❶

> **Suggested answers**
> 1 The Internet connects millions of computers together globally, forming a network in which any computer can communicate with any other computer as long as they are both connected to the Internet. The World Wide Web (or simply the Web) is a way of accessing information over the medium of the Internet.
> 2 Students' own answers.

❷ Give students three minutes to skim the passage.

> **Answer**
> Keeping track of large scientific projects; linking electronic documents about particle physics in laboratories around the world; personal social networking; political campaigning; transforming the business of doing science; publishing journals online; making links from one scientific paper to another; recruiting amateur scientists to help professionals; as an experimental laboratory; carrying out research; opening up scientific discussion; encouraging effective collaboration; reviewing / commenting on scientific articles.

Alternative treatment Ask students to work in pairs, read the title and subheading and explain in their own words what the passage will be about (*suggested answer:* How the Web started and how it is affecting science). Students should then glance at the tasks which follow. You can ask: *Which of these tasks have you done before in this book?* (*Answer:* True / False / Not Given in Unit 1).

❸ *Alternative treatment* So that students think about correct exam technique, with books closed, elicit the steps they should take with True / False / Not Given questions:

- underline the key idea in the questions;
- scan the passage to find words which echo words in the questions;
- read that section of the passage carefully to decide the answer.

With books open, you can refer students to the Exam advice in Unit 1 (p11) and Unit 4 (p39).

Suggested underlining

1 Tim Berners-Lee / famous / for his research in physics before he invented the World Wide Web (first paragraph)

2 The original intention / help manage / complex project (second paragraph)

3 Tim Berners-Lee / active in politics (third paragraph)

4 professional and amateur / work together (fourth paragraph)

5 second galaxy project / more galaxies (fourth paragraph)

6 Herbaria@home's work / reduce the effects of climate change (fourth paragraph)

❹ Students should compare their answers and show each other the words in the passage which gave them their answers.

Alternative treatment With weaker classes, tell students that Questions 1 and 2 are FALSE and TRUE. Ask them to look at the passage and say why these are the answers. They then do Questions 3–6 on their own.

Answers

1 FALSE (*a then little-known computer scientist*)

2 TRUE (*the Web was invented to deal with a specific problem. In the late 1980s, CERN was planning one of the most ambitious scientific projects ever*)

3 NOT GIVEN (Political campaigning is mentioned, but not in connection with Berners-Lee.)

4 TRUE (*permits professional scientists to recruit thousands of amateurs to give them a hand*)

5 FALSE (*classify one million images … a successor has now been launched, to classify the brightest quarter of a million*)

6 NOT GIVEN (The project tracks changes in the distribution of species in response to climate change, but no mention is made of reducing its effects.)

❺ Note-completion tasks test students' abilities to scan the passage for specific information. They reflect the type of reading activity that might be required on an undergraduate course of study. The instructions will tell them how many words they can use for each gap.

- Elicit from students the meaning of 'NO MORE THAN TWO WORDS'.

- The title should help students find the right part of the passage.

- The words in the notes will be synonymous with words in the passage, so students will have to process the meaning of both to find the correct words to complete the notes.

Tell students to scan the passage to locate the paragraphs which deal with social networking and internet use. It is essential that they realise they shouldn't read the whole passage again, so give them a minute to do this. (*Answers*: paragraphs 5 and 6)

Elicit from students that, as they read the notes, they should underline key ideas. Elicit also the type of words needed to fill each gap and why it is important to know this. (It is important students know this because it makes it easier to identify the correct words in the passage, and to produce an answer which is grammatically correct.)

Suggested answers

2 7 a characteristic of social networks

8 something sent or given to people

9 something which shows how long people spend on websites

10 visits? attention?

Tell students to underline the words they need in the passage, but also to copy the words either into the spaces provided or into their notebooks. When they have finished, tell them to read through their notes to:

- check that they make sense and reflect the ideas expressed in the passage.

- check that they have spelled the words exactly as in the passage. Many candidates lose marks by misspelling words when they copy them. (This includes the use of a singular form, when the word in the passage is plural, e.g. *size/sizes*)

- check that they have used the required number of words. Students will also lose marks if they write three words when the instructions specify no more than two, even if the three words contain the correct answer.

Answers

3 7 sizes 8 messages 9 web surfing 10 attention

❻ Short-answer questions test students' ability to scan the passage for specific information or a detail. Many of the notes for Exercise 5 above are also pertinent here. To encourage scanning, tell students not to read the whole passage again, but to find the relevant sections quickly and then read those more carefully. Set a strict time limit of four minutes.

(*Suggested words to underline*: 11 whose writing improves 12 not reviewed extensively 13 Which publication invited authors)

Answers

11 bloggers 12 scientific research 13 *Nature*

⑦ *Extension idea* As a follow-up, promote class discussion by asking the whole class:

- *What do you think is the best way of keeping in touch with close friends?*
- *How would you define a 'close' friend?*
- *How can someone become a close friend?*
- *Do you think social-networking sites help people to become close friends?*

Listening   Section 4

Tell students that Section 4 is not divided into two sections like the other three Listening sections. This means that they need to keep up with the script and the questions until the end of the test.

① *As a warmer* With books closed, ask students to work in small groups. Ask them to answer either of these questions:

- *Have you ever written an article for a magazine or newspaper?*
- *If a magazine invited you to write an article, what would you write about?*

Ask students to give details.

② Summary completion is a typical Section 4 task, which tests students' ability to pick out main ideas and details and to follow how a topic or idea is developed.

- Before answering the questions, ask: *What should you do before reading the summary? Why?* (*Answer*: Read the title – it will tell you what the listening and the summary are about. Note how many words you can use for the answers.)
- Tell students that answering the questions in Exercise 2 will help them focus on what the summary says and what information they need to listen for.

> **Answers**
> **1** noun (singular)   **2** noun (singular)
> **3** noun (singular)   **4** noun (singular)
> **5** noun (singular or plural)

Tell students also to underline words around the gaps in the summary which will help them pick out the right information when they listen.

③ 🎧 *Alternative treatment* Students at this level may find this listening challenging. You can:

- play the recording twice (although students will only hear it once in the exam itself).
- let students compare their answers and, if necessary, play it a third time for them to check.

- explain that they should not expect to be able to answer all the questions correctly; they get one mark per question, so to maximise their performance they should aim to do very well in Sections 1 and 2.

> **Answers**
> **1** photo/photograph   **2** organisation
> **3** letter   **4** local issue   **5** advertising

Extension idea 1 Students often hear and understand the correct word that they need for the answer, but spell it wrongly and therefore lose the mark. When you round up, ask students to spell the answers and where necessary, write the different spellings they have used on the board. Ask them which is the correct spelling.

Extension idea 2 Look at the recording script. Then play the recording again and ask students to underline the words they needed to complete the summary. They can then look to see how the text of the summary relates to the recording script and note the words in the summary that helped guide their listening.

Note: For classroom purposes, and because this is students' first encounter with Section 4, the recording has been divided into two parts. However, in the exam itself, unlike other parts of the Listening paper, Section 4 is not divided.

④

> **Answers**
> **1** A flow chart is a diagram showing the different stages of a process in order.
> **2, 3 6** noun (singular)   **7** noun (singular or plural)
> **8** noun (singular or plural)   **9** noun (singular)
> **10** noun (singular)

Tell students also to underline words around the gaps in the flow chart which will help them pick out the right information when they listen.

Extension idea Tell students that they are going to hear someone describing a process. In a flow chart, the separate stages in the process are shown by boxes connected by arrows. When someone is speaking, the stages will be indicated with phrases such as *firstly* or *the next stage is* (you can write these on the board as examples). Elicit other words and phrases (sequencers) which might indicate the next stage in a process (e.g. *next, then, after that, secondly, finally*). Listening out for sequencers will help students identify which stage the speaker is talking about.

⑤ 🎧 See the note for Exercise 3 above suggesting that you can play the recording more than once with students at this level and at this stage in the course.

Before students listen, ask how many words they can write in each space. (*Answer*: one)

Extension idea 1 If you did the extension idea in Exercise 4, either play the recording again or focus students on the recording script and ask them to note down the words and phrases used to indicate a new stage in the process. (Answers: *first, to start with, then, once you've written your article, then, after that, once you've got your ideas down, another thing, another, finally*)

Extension idea 2 Ask students to work in pairs and think of a process they know about which doesn't involve too much technical language (e.g. organising a party, arranging a trip, arranging to do the IELTS test). Tell them to draw a flow chart and write the steps illustrating the process, but to leave four or five gaps. They then change partners, give their new partners the gapped flow chart and take turns to describe the process to each other. They should use sequencing phrases to introduce new stages in the process. Their partners should complete the flow chart by writing words in the gap while they listen.

❻ Extension idea Ask students how to do one of these things and to describe the process.

Vocabulary
Cause, factor and *reason*

❶

Answers
1 factor   2 cause   3 reason

❷ These words are often confused because their definitions overlap. Draw attention to the dependent prepositions as a way of avoiding confusion.

Answers
cause of
major/crucial factor in
reason for
the reason why

❸

Answers
2 ~~reason~~ factor   3 ~~reasons~~ causes
4 ~~causes~~ reasons   5 ~~cause~~ reason

Extension idea Ask students to work in pairs and write three sentences of their own using *cause, factor,* and *reason* to explain why the Internet has become so successful. They then compare their sentences with another pair's.

Speaking   Parts 2 and 3

❶❷ One area on which candidates are assessed in the IELTS Speaking test is the range and appropriacy of their vocabulary in relation to the topics they are asked to talk about. Examiners note the extent to which candidates can vary the words they use and the accuracy of their choice and form of words. Therefore, it is a good idea for students in their minute of preparation for Part 2 to also think of and note down suitable vocabulary on the topic.

When students have discussed the vocabulary in the box, elicit definitions or examples of any words/phrases you think they may have problems with.

Answers
In this case they could use any of the vocabulary in the box, depending on how they use their favourite website.

❸ Extension idea Students usually do these activities better the second time and learn a lot from the opportunity to repeat the activity. When they have finished, ask them to think for a minute (and discuss with their partners) how they could have done the activity better. Then ask them to change partners and do the activity again (using the same prompt card) incorporating their improvements.

❹ In Part 3, the examiner chooses a set of questions on a particular theme. The examiner will use these questions to guide the conversation, and will ask additional questions to help candidates produce extended answers. Tell your students that the questions will gradually get harder as Part 3 progresses.

After students have discussed the three answers, round up with the whole class to reach the conclusions in the suggested answer.

Suggested answers
Answer A doesn't answer the question – the speaker talks about himself and does not give a general answer; the answer is irrelevant. The speaker does not show that he has understood the question.
Answer B is the best – it is a quite long, detailed answer to the question, which demonstrates a range of well-expressed vocabulary and ideas.
Answer C is too short and doesn't get to grips with the question or even demonstrate understanding of *how?*

Alternative treatment Write these questions on the board. Students then judge each answer according to these criteria.
• *Does it answer the question?*

- *Does it show the candidate has understood the question?*
- *Are the ideas linked together naturally?*
- *Does it show a range of relevant vocabulary?*
- *Does the answer include reasons and examples?*
- *Is the answer long enough? Is the candidate demonstrating an ability to speak English?*

Extension idea Ask students to work alone and think of their own answer to the question. They then work in small groups and take turns to give their answers. Ask them to decide which answer was best and why. They can use the criteria from the alternative treatment above.

❺ Tell students they are discussing how best to answer these questions at the moment, rather than doing exam practice. Encourage them also to think of appropriate vocabulary for their answers.

❻ Tell students that it is better to say they are not certain about an answer and suggest different possibilities rather than say they don't know. They can use words like *maybe* and *perhaps* to suggest different possibilities.

> **Answers**
> **1** The second one
> **2** Reasons: *for their jobs*; *too much time sitting down*; *saves time*
> Examples: *young people who should be studying instead*; *chatting to friends*; *instead of a telephone or … going to the library.*
> **3** *Well, I'm not sure*; *perhaps*; *Maybe*; *so, I think it depends.*

Note This is a good moment to do the Pronunciation section on Chunking on page 43, which is partly based on Elena's answer in Exercise 6.

❼ Ask students to change partners for this exercise. The student who is listening can give feedback using the criteria in Exercise 4 above (alternative treatment).

❽ *Alternative treatment* Give one student in each pair more realistic exam practice by asking them to close their books to answer the questions, while the other student (taking the role of examiner) reads the questions aloud. When they have finished, they change roles and repeat.

Pronunciation
Chunking

❶ 🎧 Grouping words together in chunks and pausing naturally between the chunks is an essential part of fluency and natural speech rhythms. Pausing in places where it is natural to pause helps the listener to understand. In the IELTS Speaking test, the examiner will listen to how effectively a candidate handles rhythm and chunking. As with other features of pronunciation, students need to show that they have a reasonable grasp of this in order to achieve a mid-band score.

Play the recording and elicit that the pauses come between words grouped together for meaning. As in any language, pauses will come while the speaker searches for the most appropriate word, or decides what to say next.

> **Suggested answers**
> Well, / I think it helps people / in quite a lot of ways, / for instance / to get information, / or to book air tickets, / it helps people to study / and to do research / for their homework and their studies / or even to get advice / about how to study.

❷

> **Answers**
> Well, I'm not sure. / Some people do perhaps, / for example young people who should be studying instead, / but a lot of people use the Internet for their jobs / or for other things. / Maybe too much time chatting to friends, / not enough time doing other things. / Too much time sitting down. / But many people leave the Internet connected all day / because they use it instead of a telephone for messages / or instead of going to the library, so I think it depends. / For some things, / it saves time.

❸ When each student has finished, ask them to change partners and do the exercise again.

Extension idea Ask students to note down the main ideas from Elena's answer and then, working in pairs, take turns to answer the question using their notes rather than reading.

Writing   Task 2

In Writing Task 2, candidates are expected to answer every part of the question. Explain that some questions have only one part, while others have more than one. If students read the question too quickly and fail to notice something they must include, they will lose marks for content, so this early stage of preparation is extremely important.

❶ *As a warmer* With books closed, ask students to work in small groups.

- Ask them to think of some good news they have heard on the news recently.

- Ask: *Why do you think so much news you hear or read is bad news? Do you think this affects the way people see the world? Does it give a realistic impression of what is happening in the world?*

Ask students to do the exercise in the book. Elicit why it's important to analyse the question before planning. (*Answer*: to make sure the answer is relevant and answers the question exactly – irrelevant answers lose marks.)

> **Suggested answers**
> limit / bad news / discourages / activities / little risk / To what extent / agree / disagree / reasons / examples
> Students should write about a, c, e and f.

2 Many students find the hardest part of writing an essay is the opening paragraph. Once they have written this, everything follows more easily. Tell students that:

- it is essential to write a good opening paragraph, as first impressions are important.

- there is no one 'right' way to write an opening paragraph, but the paragraphs in this exercise indicate three possible right ways.

> **Answers**
> 1 c   2 a   3 b

3 Point out that although it is fine for the opening paragraph not to state the writer's opinion (as in Exercise 3 paragraph 2), students must make sure that somewhere in their answer their opinion is absolutely clear to the reader. If not, they aren't answering the question completely and will lose marks.

> **Answers**
> a ✓   c ✓   d ✓

Extension idea 1 When students have finished, ask:

- *Why is it good to write a short opening paragraph?* (*Answer*: It is an introduction to the subject and will leave more space for answering the question in detail.)

- *Why is it often good to state your opinion at the beginning?* (*Answer*: The reader gets a clear idea of where you stand. The rest of the essay is likely to express ideas which support your opinion.)

- *Why is it important not to repeat the words from the question?* (*Answer*: Examiners ignore sentences and clauses that are copied from the rubric and they do not include these when they count the number of words in the answer. Warn students that they could go under the 250-word count if they do this.)

Extension idea 2 Ask students to write an opening paragraph for the writing activity in Exercise 8 using one of the paragraphs in this exercise as a model. They then work in groups and exchange paragraphs. The other students read what they have written and decide whether their paragraph fits description a, b, or c from Exercise 3.

4 Draw students' attention to the Exam overview on page 7, which deals with marking criteria for the writing task. Mention that it is important to plan the essay before starting. Many candidates lose marks because they start writing their answers straightaway. As a result, their answers lack a clear overall structure and the reader may have difficulty following the argument.

> **Answers**
> 1 b   2 d   3 e   4 a

5 In addition to the overall structure, students will gain marks in the exam for linking their ideas logically (and coherently) within and across paragraphs and for more complex use of language. In fact, students cannot expect to score above Band 5 for Grammar if they do not use a mixture of simple and complex sentence forms. Exercises 6 and 7 work on improving these features.

Elicit that the highlighted words and phrases are used to contrast two facts or ideas, and that using these improves the complexity of sentences. IELTS students often confuse the grammatical usage of these words and phrases.

If your students need, go through the Language reference on page 103.

> **Answers**
> 1 *However, On the other hand*
> 2 *even though, although*

6

> **Answers**
> 2 e   3 d   4 b   5 c   6 a

Extension idea Ask students to work in pairs and say which statements in this exercise they agree with and which they disagree with and why.

Note This is a good moment to do the Key grammar section on articles on page 45.

7

> **Suggested underlining**
> too much attention / lives and relationships of celebrities / more time / reporting / ordinary people / To what extent / agree / disagree / reasons / examples

8 *Alternative treatment* With books closed, you can reinforce students' knowledge of good exam technique. Elicit the stages they should go through before writing an essay. (*Answers*: 1 underlining the key points in the task; 2 analysing the question; 3 brainstorming ideas and making notes; 4 writing a plan)

9 If students did Extension idea 2 in exercise 4, they can use the same paragraph to start their essay. When they have finished, ask them to work in pairs and compare their plans.

Tell students to follow their plans carefully when they write – examiners notice when essays are not clearly structured. Point out that in the exam, they would have about 40 minutes for the whole task including planning, but at this stage in the course it is more important to produce a good answer than to stick to the time limit.

Sample answer

Famous people such as footballers and actors are often on the television and in newspapers. Ordinary people, on the other hand, are rarely in the news. I believe that this is a good thing and something that the public prefer.

People enjoy getting news about celebrities because their lives are exciting. When they read about their homes or see the clothes they wear, many people want to own similar things. So it makes them feel good to dream about the possibilities. Similarly, when people read about the achievements of celebrities, it gives them a desire to do well in life too.

Some people say that ordinary people can also have interesting lives. They may suggest, for example, that a fireman who rescues many people from a burning building or a manager whose business has profited should be in the news as much as a footballer or singer. After all, many celebrities don't actually do very much and some of them are only famous because they are married to other famous people.

However, I don't think the general public wants to read about ordinary workers very often. They may enjoy one article but there is nothing to encourage them to read more. If a newspaper did decide to write a story about someone unknown, readers might feel that their own lives are just as newsworthy and wonder why the story has been told.

It is certainly true that the public are always hungry for gossip and excitement. In the end, the media have to make money by attracting readers and viewers. For this, they need sensational stories and attractive pictures, and only celebrities can provide these.

(275 words)

Key grammar
Articles

1 When students have finished this exercise, it is a good idea to reinforce it by going through the rules in the Language reference on page 104.

Answers
2 the world   3 the media
4 the safest ways   5 a right
6 people/businesses   7 people/businesses

Extension idea After going through the Language reference, ask students to add an example of their own to each rule.

2 Tell students that as IELTS candidates make frequent mistakes with articles, they should be especially careful about using them correctly in their writing.

Answers
2 in ~~the~~ society   3 ~~the~~ computers   4 **The** Internet
5 ~~the~~ people   6 ~~the~~ information   7 ~~the~~ books
8 ~~a~~ **the** best school

Vocabulary and grammar review Unit 3

Answers

Vocabulary

1 2 find out   3 taught   4 studied   5 know
6 studying / to study   7 learned/learnt   8 knew

Grammar

2 2 Have you decided   3 wrote   4 came from
5 have been waiting / have waited   6 felt
7 has been travelling / has travelled
8 has never read

3 2 Between   3 in   4 over   5 by   6 to   7 From   8 of
9 in   10 at

Vocabulary and grammar review Unit 4

Answers

Vocabulary

1 2 chat   3 visit   4 keep   5 go   6 download

2 2 cause   3 reason   4 reasons   5 cause(s)   6 factor

Grammar

❸ **2** Although / Even though   **3** although / even though
4 However   **5** However / On the other hand

❹ **2** a   **3** An   **4** the   **5** –   **6** the/–   **7** The   **8** the   **9** –/
the   **10** The/–   **11** a   **12** –   **13** the   **14** the   **15** the

Unit 4 photocopiable activity:
The internet debate

Time: 45 minutes

Objectives

- To encourage oral fluency in a debate format
- To practise chunking words and phrases when speaking
- To practise brainstorming ideas for and against a topic
- To revise Internet-related vocabulary and phrases
- To revise the use of linking words: *however, although, even though, on the other hand*

Before class

You will need one photocopy of the activity page on page 46 for each student.

In class

❶ Ask students to work in pairs to do the matching task, which revises vocabulary and grammar taught in Unit 4. Check answers with the whole class. Then give the pairs time to tick the sentences they agree with and put a question mark next to the others, before discussing how the statements compare to their own experiences.

| **1** h | **2** d | **3** g | **4** b | **5** f | **6** e | **7** a | **8** c |

❷ Tell students they are going to have a class debate. If you have more than ten students in the class, you should first put students into two or more debating groups of up to ten. You should then divide each debating group into two equal teams: 'for' and 'against'. Focus students on the debate topic. Tell them to discuss the points relevant to their side of the debate and brainstorm two more of their own. They should come up with as many examples and reasons as they can to back up the points. To help students to understand the brainstorming process, you may wish to give a brief demonstration, by eliciting arguments 'for' and 'against' the following statement: *University education should be compulsory for all citizens.*

- The teams then take turns to speak for two minutes on each point. It is up to each team to decide who will speak on which point, and

whether they will present as individuals or in pairs, but every student should have an equal chance to speak at length. Encourage teams to rehearse their speeches as a group before they present to the class. Remind them to think about chunking when they rehearse so as to sound clearer and more natural.

- Once all the points have been covered, conduct a class vote to see whether the motion has been carried or defeated. Encourage students to vote honestly based on the arguments they have heard, rather than just for their own team.

- After the voting, conduct a feedback session, based on any errors you may have noticed during the presentations, especially in the use of linking words. Write these on the board for students to discuss and correct in pairs.

Extension idea 1 If your students enjoyed the internet debate, you could cover the topic below in a subsequent class. Follow the same procedure above.

Social networking sites have a positive effect on society.

For

1 Websites such as Facebook allow people to develop and keep important friendships.

2 People from different countries can communicate more easily.

3 These sites make it easier to share music and other cultural interests.

Against

1 Chatting online will never be as healthy as meeting friends face to face.

2 Social-networking sites do not provide information which is useful for study or work purposes.

3 Some people become addicted to social networking, which may affect their performance at work or at school.

Extension idea 2 As a follow-up to either of the debates, set the writing task below. Remind students to use the points from both sides of the debates, as well as linking words.

The Internet has come to dominate every aspect of human life. Despite its undoubted benefits, the Internet has caused more problems that it has solved.

To what extent do you agree or disagree?

Give reasons for your answer and include any relevant examples from your own knowledge or experience.

Write at least 250 words.

The internet debate

❶ Work in pairs. Match phrases and sentences 1–8 with their endings a–h.
Then discuss how similar these statements are to your own experience of using the internet.

1   Even though I spend at least five hours a day online,

2   I spend a lot of time on social-networking sites,

3   I think it's important for parents to stop their children visiting

4   I don't use the internet to download

5   I rarely find that browsing

6   I never use the internet for chatting

7   I really enjoy going shopping at weekends.

8   I think the internet is a good source of information.

a   However, I find that shopping online is more convenient.

b   music because I prefer to buy CDs.

c   On the other hand, some websites are not reliable.

d   although I don't think I'm addicted to them.

e   with friends because I prefer talking to them in person.

f   the internet helps me to find the information I need.

g   websites which are not suitable for them.

h   I'm not sure I make the best use of the internet.

❷ Work in groups. Debate the following topic.

The internet causes more problems than it solves.

For

1   Spending too much time online makes people become isolated from each other.

2   The internet is a much less reliable source of information than printed books.

3   Internet shopping will never be as easy or enjoyable as buying products in shops.

4

5

Against

1   The internet considerably increases our access to a huge range of information.

2   People can use the internet to share and develop ideas more efficiently.

3   Online business is much quicker and more efficient than traditional business.

4

5

Vocabulary extension

Unit 4

Abbreviations: n/pln = noun / plural noun; v = verb; adj = adjective; adv = adverb; p = phrase; T/I = transitive/intransitive; C/U = countable/uncountable

advertisement *n* [C] a picture, short film, song, etc. which tries to persuade people to buy a product or service

advertising *n* [U] the business of trying to persuade people to buy products or services

be in the news *p* If something is in the news, it is reported in news reports.

broadcast the news *p* to have the news on a TV or radio programme

comedy *n* [C] entertainment such as a film, play or TV programme which is funny

current affairs documentary *n* [C] a film or TV programme about political, social or economic events that are happening now

entertainment *n* [U] shows, films, television or other performances or activities that people enjoy

headlines *pln* the main stories in the news

interview a politician *p* to ask a politician questions for an article, TV or radio programme, etc.

investigate a crime *p* to try to discover who committed a crime

local newspaper *n* [C] a newspaper that is sold in a particular area of a country and mainly reports events in that area

national newpaper *n* [C] a newspaper that is sold in the whole of a country and reports events in the whole country and abroad

newspaper readers *pln* people who read a newspaper

publish a story *n* [C] to print a story in a newspaper, magazine, etc.

radio station *n* [C] a company which sends out radio broadcasts or a part of a company that sends out particular types of broadcasts

reality show *n* [C] a television programme about ordinary people filmed in real situations, rather than actors

report an accident *p* to give information about an accident in a news article or broadcast

satellite TV *n* [C] television programmes that are sent using satellites (=devices sent into space that travel round the Earth)

sports magazine *n* [C] a magazine about sport

television audience *n* [C] the people who watch a TV programme

television channel *n* [C] one of the groups of TV programmes broadcast by a particular company

television series *n* [C] a set of TV programmes about the same subject or using the same characters

the latest news *n* [U] the most recent things that are reported in the news

turn off *v* T to stop a piece of equipment such as a TV or radio working by pressing a button or moving a switch

turn on *v* T to make a piece of equipment such as a TV or radio start working by pressing a button or moving a switch

watch television *p* to look at programmes on the TV

❶ **Complete the paragraph by writing one word from the box in each gap. There are four extra words you do not need to use.**

analysis	argument	assignment	data	experiments	findings
hypothesis	investigation	journal	laboratory	proof	research	~~steps~~

The scientific method often consists of the following **(0)** .... *steps* .... First, scientists identify a problem or area they want to **(1)** .... or investigate. They then examine existing information or **(2)** .... on the subject and propose a theory or **(3)** ....
They may then carry out further investigation in order to collect more information. They may also conduct **(4)** .... in order to test their theory. While we often think of scientists working in a **(5)** ...., they may also do a lot of work using a computer or outside in the field. Once scientists have completed these stages, they then conduct an **(6)** ....
of all the information and modify their theory accordingly. A final stage is often that they publish their **(7)** .... (in other words, what they have discovered) in a scientific
(8) ....

❷ **Choose the best alternative (A, B or C) for each of these sentences.**

0 In his first job he .... *C* .... natural sciences to first-year students.
   A learned   **B** studied   **C** taught

1 If you're not sure what the process is called, you can .... by looking in an online encyclopedia.
   A learn it   **B** know it   **C** find it out

2 Chan-juan wants to .... how to drive, so she's starting lessons next week.
   A learn   **B** study   **C** find out

3 Nasr is planning to .... medicine at university.
   A learn   **B** study   **C** find out

4 The main .... why Sasha came to this country was to learn English.
   A cause   **B** reason   **C** factor

5 A person's weight may be influenced by their diet and their genes, but exercise is also a ....
   A cause   **B** reason   **C** factor

6 .... he is an excellent researcher, he has never published an article.
   A However   **B** Although   **C** On the other hand

7 She handed in her assignment without apologising to her teacher .... it was two weeks late.
   A even though   **B** however   **C** but

8 I enjoy watching films. ...., I never download them from the Internet.
   A Although   **B** Even though   **C** However

❸ **Complete these sentences by putting the verbs in brackets into the correct tense: past simple, present perfect simple or present perfect continuous.**

0 Darwin ....*spent*........ (spend) more than 20 years working on *On the Origin of Species* before its publication in 1859.

1 Farouk .... (study) so hard recently that we've hardly seen him.

2 Scientists .... (conduct) a national study into people's sleeping habits which they hope to complete in the autumn.

3 Joyce .... (live) in Italy for over ten years before moving to Switzerland in 1915.

4 Takeshi is unable to give his presentation this morning as his computer .... (break) down.

5 I .... (not see) the film yet, but I hope to see it this weekend.

6 I .... (speak) to your supervisor yesterday and he says your work is fine.

❹ **Complete this paragraph by writing *the, a, an* or – if no article is needed.**

Before **(0)** ....*the*........ World Wide Web was invented, **(0)** ....–............ scientists had difficulty communicating on **(1)** .... complex projects, especially if they were working in **(2)** .... different parts of **(3)** .... world. **(4)** .... ability to share **(5)** .... information instantaneously is **(6)** .... enormous advantage because it allows, for example, **(7)** .... scientist working in Peru to work closely on **(8)** .... same project as **(9)** .... colleagues working in **(10)** .... university in India.

❺ **Complete these sentences, writing the correct preposition (*by, for, with, to,* etc.) in each gap. For some questions, more than one answer is possible.**

The graph shows the number **(0)** ....*of*........ visits per month to a website **(1)** .... 2011. During the period **(2)** .... January to March, visits rose **(3)** .... 27 percent to a total of 9,589.

(4) .... April and June visits remained steady **(5)** .... just over 9,600.

(6) .... July there was a 10 percent fall **(7)** .... visits.

During the next seven months, visits fell **(8)** .... a level in December of about 8,000.

Unit 5 The world in our hands

Unit objectives

- **Listening Section 1:** note completion and table completion
- **Vocabulary:** *nature, the environment* and *the countryside; tourist* and *tourism;* words and phrases related to environmental change
- **Reading Section 2:** introduction to matching-information tasks; matching features; summary completion
- **Speaking Parts 2 and 3:** preparing notes for Part 2; using adjectives to improve vocabulary scores; generalising in Part 3
- **Pronunciation:** using sentence stress for emphasis
- **Writing Task 1:** describing diagrams; paragraphing; sequencing
- **Key grammar:** the passive

Starting off

❶ *As a warmer* With books closed, ask students to work in small groups and give them three minutes to brainstorm problems related to the environment. They then open their books to work on the ones listed.

> **Suggested answers**
> **1** d   **2** a   **3** b   **4** e   **5** c

Extension idea Ask students: *Which of these are problems in your country/region? Why? What is being done to solve the problem?*

❷ In exercises 1 and 2, students may have problems with some of the vocabulary. If possible, try to elicit explanations. You can also hand out the photocopiable Word List on page 59 of this book to help.

> **Answers**
> **1** c   **2** d   **3** b   **4** a

Listening   Section 1

❶ You can help students by telling them that *eco-* is short for *ecological*. Ask: *In what ways are tourism or going on holiday bad for the environment?* (*Suggested answers*: air travel or other means of travel cause pollution; large numbers of people visiting places of natural beauty tend to be harmful to those places;

tourists require modern hotels and restaurants which may spoil places, etc.).

Eco-holidays are holidays which do as little damage to the environment as possible, and where possible, the holiday-makers participate in things to improve or protect the environment. It may be possible to draw on the experiences some students have of eco-holidays which are available in their own countries.

❷ Elicit why it's a good idea to predict what type of information you need first. (*Answer*: it helps focus on the question before listening; you know what you are listening for.) Also elicit the strategies that help students judge the type of information that is needed. (*Answer*: underlining key words and looking at the words before and after the gap.) Ask:

- *How many words can you use to answer each question?* (*Answer*: one or two)
- *What else can you use?* (*Answer*: a number)

❸ 🎧 Play this section just once, as in the exam, then ask students to compare answers with a partner. Play the recording again to check answers.

> **Answers**
> **1** two / 2 weeks   **2** 1,750   **3** discount
> **4** (travel) insurance   **5** vegetarian meals   **6** visa

Explain that abbreviations are acceptable (e.g. *wks*), but encourage students to write words in full in case they make a mistake.

❹ Ask: *How are the instructions for Questions 7–10 different from the instructions for Questions 1–6?* (*Answer*: you write one word, no number.) Stress that it is important to check what you can write in each gap before listening. When students have looked at the table, they should compare the information they think they will need with a partner.

❺ 🎧 Play the recording once only, then allow students to compare their answers with their partner.

> **Answers**
> **7** tree   **8** (local) family   **9** school   **10** cars

Alternative treatment Play the recording once only (students won't hear it a second time in the exam). In order to emphasise the need to concentrate on listening for the details required in the task and not panic if they don't understand something, ask:

- *Did you understand everything that was said?* (*Suggested answer*: students at this level needn't understand every word, but they should try to pick out the signals and clues which flag up the words they need for their answers.)

- *Was it possible to answer the questions without understanding everything?* (*Suggested answer*: the IELTS exam is designed to measure students' abilities over a wide range of levels, so students should expect some questions which are very challenging. However, they should find Listening Section 1 easier than other sections.)

- *What should you do when you don't understand everything you hear?* (*Answer*: continue listening for the details you need using the words in the questions as a guide.)

6 Before students answer the questions, ask: *In what ways are each of the holidays you heard about eco-holidays?*

Extension idea 1 Ask students:
- *Do you think it's important to have holidays? Why (not)? What for you would be the ideal holiday?*

Extension idea 2 If your students all come from the same area, ask them to work in small groups and discuss:
- *What sort of eco-holiday could visitors have if they came to your region?*
Or if eco-holidays already exist:
- *What sort of eco-holiday works best in your region?*

Vocabulary
Nature, the environment or *the countryside*?
Tourist or *tourism*?

1 *As a warmer* With books closed, write these words on the board: *nature, the environment, the countryside*. Ask students:

- *Which would you use to refer to land which is outside cities and towns, land which is probably green with trees and plants growing there?* (*Answer: the countryside*)

- *Which would you use to refer to animals, plants, birds and other living things?* (*Answer: nature*)

Next, ask students to work in pairs and supply their own definition for *the environment*. (*Suggested answer*: everything around us where animals and plants live) Then ask students to match the words with the definitions in their books.

> **Answers**
> **1** b **2** c **3** a **4** e **5** d

2 Using the example, elicit why *the environment* is correct in this gap. (*Answer*: We talk about the environment when we refer to the natural world which people damage.)

> **Answers**
> **2** nature **3** countryside **4** tourists **5** tourist **6** tourism

3 Tell students to be careful when using these words in their writing or speaking, as IELTS candidates often make mistakes with them.

> **Answers**
> **2** ~~nature~~ environment **3** ~~tourists~~ tourism **4** ✓ **5** ~~nature~~ countryside

Extension idea Ask students to write three sentences of their own using these words.

Reading   Section 2

1 *As a warmer* With books closed, tell students they are going to read about a form of renewable energy.

- Ask them to work in pairs and brainstorm different forms of renewable energy (e.g. solar power). (*Suggested answers*: wind power, wave power, geothermal energy from the Earth's core, hydropower from dams and rivers)

- Ask students: *Which type of renewable energy do you think would be best for your country? Why?*

Still with books closed, and to encourage good exam technique, elicit what students' first steps should be when dealing with a reading passage. (*Answers*: look at the title and subheading; glance through the different tasks they have to do; skim the passage to get a general idea.)

With books open, ask students to do the exercise.

> **Suggested answers**
> **1** The title and subheading of the article lead readers to make the connections that the Sahara Desert may produce solar energy to satisfy Europe's energy needs and that this will be 'green'.
> **2** Students' own answers

Elicit what 'green' means in this context. (*Answer*: environmentally friendly)

❷ To develop scanning skills, give students a time limit of three minutes. When they finish, ask them to compare answers in small groups.

> **Suggested answers**
> (any three of these): (dust), expensive; building installations; remote terrain, need for cables under the Mediterranean; need for new electrical grids; convincing governments and companies it's worth doing

❸ Matching information is a typical Reading Section 2 activity.

- While matching headings will focus on the global idea or purpose of each paragraph, matching information asks students to locate specific information which may be embedded somewhere in any of the paragraphs.

- Students should look carefully at the instructions and the opening of each question, which tell them what to look for. Elicit the difference between the type of information required for Question 1 and that required for Question 4 by focusing on the opening words of the questions: *mention* and *description*.

If the rubric 'You may use any letter more than once' is present, it means that sometimes a paragraph may contain more than one piece of information (which is asked for). Other paragraphs may not contain any of the information required.

- This task type tests students' abilities to skim, scan and read in detail.

- The words in the questions will not repeat words from the passage, but will contain a rephrasing or summary of an idea.

Students may have problems doing this task because they haven't read the instructions carefully. This exercise mainly concentrates on understanding the instructions.

> **Answers**
> **1** No   **2** Yes
> **Suggested underlining:**
> **2** quantity of power
> **3** how to convince organisations
> **4** Sahara at present
> **5** costs of two different energy sources

❹ Especially with weaker classes, help students by asking them to concentrate on paragraph A: it contains one of the answers/pieces of information. (*answer*: 4).

- Tell students to tick off the information as they find it and to underline the words in the paragraphs which give them the answer.

- Remind them that if there is nothing clearly stated which gives them the answer, they should look somewhere else.

- Remind them that these are five out of 13 questions, so they should limit their time to a maximum of eight minutes. Students could do this task in pairs.

> **Answers**
> **1** E   **2** B   **3** G   **4** A   **5** E

❺ Matching features tests students' ability to scan the passage for options (in this case, names of organisations) and then read that part of the passage carefully to find the information which goes with each name. The names are listed in the same order as in the passage.

Students should read the instructions carefully. Sometimes the box contains fewer options than the number of questions. In this case, they will need to use some letters more than once (see Student's book Unit 7 on page 72). In other cases, the box may contain more options than the number of questions, so students will not need to use all the letters.

(*Suggested underlining*: 6 set a time for achieving an objective 7 successful small-scale projects will demonstrate that larger projects are possible 8 a number of renewable energy projects under construction 9 already experimenting / other parts of the world)

> **Answers**
> **6** F (*has passed a law that aids investors who help the continent reach its goal of getting 20% of its power from renewable energy by 2020*)
>
> **7** G (*thinks companies should begin transmitting small amounts of solar power as soon as the North African plants begin operating, by linking a few cable lines under the Med … If it can be shown that power from the Sahara can be produced profitably, he says, companies and governments will soon jump in.*)
>
> **8** E (*is building one solar-thermal plant in Algeria and another in Morocco*)
>
> **9** A (*is testing solar plants in Oman and the United Arab Emirates*)

Extension idea Students read around the unused options and state why they are wrong (you could do this as part of the feedback).

❻ Summary completion tests students' ability to scan the passage to find where the subject of the summary is dealt with – in this case they need to find the paragraph on Concentrating Solar Power (*answer*: paragraph C).

- Once students have found it, they should look at the summary to see what type of words they need and what information, and then read the paragraph carefully to fill the gaps.

> **Answers**
> **10** plural noun   **11** singular noun
> **12** noun (a place)   **13** noun

- You can elicit the steps from students, as they have already followed these for several other tasks: look at the title, scan to locate the part of the text, and decide what type of words are needed.

- Students should take particular care to copy the words they need exactly as they are printed in the passage (words with double letters such as *mirrors*, *depressions* and *irrigation* are easily misspelled).

- Encourage students to read the completed summary to check that it makes sense, reflects what they have understood from the passage, and is grammatically correct.

- When students have finished, ask them to work in pairs to compare their answers. Then round up answers with the whole class and check spelling. Many marks are lost at this level by IELTS candidates miscopying words from the passage.

> **Answers**
> Paragraph C
> **10** mirrors   **11** steam   **12** depressions
> **13** irrigation

❼ Extension idea To give students practice at speaking at length, when they have finished, ask them to change groups and present a summary of their answers to their new group.

Speaking   Parts 2 and 3

❶ As a warmer Ask students to discuss in small groups: *Where do people go at weekends in your country (or region) when the weather is good? What do they do there?*

When students look at the exercise in the book, remind them that it is a good idea to make notes on all the points on the prompt card.

❷

> **Answers**
> **2** fantastic   **3** wonderful   **4** lovely   **5** warm
> **6** spectacular   **7** unspoilt   **8** fresh

At the end of the recording, draw students' attention to the two rounding-off questions that the examiner asks and the brief nature of Jamila's responses. Point out that if students have spoken for two minutes, they do

not need to give long responses to these rounding-off questions.

Extension idea Ask: *Are the adjectives positive or negative? Why?* (*Answer:* Positive – Jamila is talking about a beautiful place.) Tell students to think of adjectives they can add to the notes they made in Exercise 1.

Note: This is a good moment to do the Pronunciation section on sentence stress on page 54, which is based on Jamila's answer.

❸ Before they speak, remind students that they should try to use their own words, not just repeat the words on the prompt card. Give students some time to think how they can do this. Ask the student who is listening to give feedback on the following points (you can write them on the board).

- *Did your partner deal with all the points on the prompt card?*

- *What adjectives did he/she use? Did he/she stress them?*

- *Did your partner speak for two minutes?*

❹ Remind students that the questions in Part 3 are connected to the topic of Part 2.

- Ask: *Is the question asking in general, or is it asking about a particular place?*

- Ask students to brainstorm ideas to answer the question of what attracts tourists to a place. Give two minutes.

Alternative treatment If your class doesn't have many ideas, you can elicit the following suggested answers: it has a good climate; it's a beautiful or interesting place; there are plenty of things to do; it's relaxing; it's famous; lots of other people visit it; it's easy or cheap to get there; it's exotic or unusual; it's safe; the people are friendly; it has monuments, ruins and museums; it has good hotels; it has good food and restaurants, etc.

Note: Point out to students that they should not include all these ideas in their answer – there isn't time.

❺

> **Answers**
> **1** three ideas: go to well-known tourist destinations for safety; choose places with plenty of hotels for good accommodation and lots of things to do; choose places where weather will be good
> **2** students' own answers

❻ Tell students that they will be asked questions like this, which require a very general answer. This exercise provides ways of giving one. Students can also add a more particular example to support their generalisations.

❼ As noted in the Teacher's Book Unit 4, examiners have several sets of questions for Part 3. Depending on a candidate's performance, they will start with one (an easier) set of questions and move on to a more challenging set. The second set of questions here is designed to be more challenging: the concepts are more difficult to understand; the ideas students will have to express are more complex and may require more complex grammar and lower-frequency vocabulary. It's likely that weaker students will not be asked such challenging questions in the exam.

Alternative treatment With weaker classes which may struggle with the set on the environment, you can:

* elicit environmental problems mentioned earlier in the unit. Ask students to look back to Starting off.

* elicit whose reponsibility by asking if it is ordinary people (how?), governments, or other organisations. Ask students to think of reasons why each of these might be responsible.

❽ To give students a feel of how the actual speaking test will be, they should take turns to answer all the questions.

Extension idea The student asking the questions and listening could give feedback at the end. Suggest these criteria:

* *What did your partner do well?*
* *What could they do better?*
* *Did they use some of the vocabulary you have learnt in this unit?*

Once they have finished giving feedback, they change roles.

* Get general feedback from the whole class, including where they had problems and how they could deal with them.

Pronunciation
Sentence stress 2

❶ 🎧 Students worked on sentence stress in Unit 1. Elicit what words are usually stressed (*Answer*: words which are important for the meaning). If necessary, ask students to refer back to Unit 1 on page 13. For answers, see the underlined words in the script.

❷ You should be able to elicit these answers. Point out that here, the words with the most stress are the ones which express the speaker's attitude to what she is saying.

❸ *Extension idea* Ask students to think of two or three sentences containing positive adjectives which they could use when talking about the topic on the prompt card in Speaking Part 2. They then take turns to say the sentences to their partners.

Writing   Task 1

❶ *As a warmer* With books closed, tell students they are going to look at diagrams showing how wave power can be used to make electricity. Tell them to approach a diagram in the same way as they do a graph or chart (i.e. to highlight the key stages in the information and add details to support them). First, ask: *What are the advantages of wave power?* (*Suggested answers*: It's renewable; it doesn't pollute; and it's possible in countries with sea coasts.)

* Before answering the questions in the book, ask students to look at both diagrams and elicit the meaning of: *flow*, *turbine*, *chambers* and *output*.

* When students have answered the questions, ask them to compare their ideas in groups of four. Round up with the whole class.

❷

> **Answers**
> 2 enters 3 rises 4 passes 5 connected
> 6 sucked 7 turns 8 installed
> 9 produced/generated 10 produced/generated

❸ Remind students that it is important to divide their writing into paragraphs. Each should have a specific purpose.

> **Suggested answers**
> ... placed. //
> The machine ... a generator. //
> When the wave ... the turbine. //
> The machine ... to install. //
> In general ...
>
> **Paragraph 1:** Introduction: what the diagrams show
> **Paragraph 2:** The first part of the process
> **Paragraph 3:** The second part of the process
> **Paragraph 4:** Where the machine can be located
> **Paragraph 5:** A general conclusion.

Note: This is a good moment to do the Key grammar section on the passive.

❹❺

Answers		
introduces the first part of the process	**explains that one thing happens after another**	**explains that two things happen simultaneously**
• the process starts when • first • In the first stage of the process	• as a result • when the wave goes down • as a consequence • following this • In the next stage • next • then	• as • at the same time • meanwhile

Extension idea Ask students to add an extra column with phrases which introduce the last stage in a process. You should be able to elicit these phrases: *finally, lastly* (but not *at last* which suggests impatience to finish something which has gone on too long).

❻ Before doing the exercises in the book, elicit the meanings of these words from the diagrams (which should be clear from the context): *blades*, *sensor* and *landscape*.

When students have written their plans, they should change partners and compare ideas with someone from another pair. Encourage them to amend their plans when they think it is a good idea.

Alternative treatment With weaker classes, round up by eliciting what information and comparisons they have extracted from the two diagrams.

You may wish to give the final writing task for homework.

• Now that students are getting closer to the exam, ask them to time themselves and write their answers in 20 minutes. Discourage them from doing the task in less than 20 minutes, as they will produce an inferior piece of work.

Extension idea You could photocopy and hand out the following sample answer which has the paragraphs in the wrong order. Ask students to put the paragraphs in the correct order. (*Answers:* 1 C, 2 A, 3 D, 4 B)

> **Sample answer**
> The diagrams explain where wind turbines should be placed and what they look like.
>
> According to the diagrams, there are three possible positions for a turbine. A large industrial turbine would be built high up on a hillside where the wind is strongest and these turbines can produce 1.5 megawatts of power. On the other hand, smaller turbines that produce about 100 kilowatts of power for domestic use can be found on rooftops. A third possible position is in the sea. Here, there is less impact on the countryside but winds can still be very strong.
>
> While the locations may be different, the turbines themselves all have the same special shape. They consist of a tall tower made of strong steel and on top of this there are three blades made of fibreglass or wood. The turbines are controlled by a computer which can alter the direction and angle of the blades according to the information it receives from a sensor.
>
> Clearly most wind turbines are very large and all turbines need to be exposed to a lot of wind.

Key grammar
The passive

❶

> **Answer**
> is pushed

❷

> **Answers**
> can be placed; is connected; is sucked; can be placed; can be installed; is generated/produced; can be placed; can be generated/produced

❸

> **Answer**
> b and c

❹ Make sure students realise that they have to use the verb *to be* in the same tense as the original active verb that they are transforming.

- Use the example to point out or elicit that *They* in the original sentence is used in the active because we don't know who or what does this.

- Use the example to also point out that the idea here is more naturally expressed in the passive. You can point out that the passive is a more natural way to express all the meanings in these sentences.

- Do question 2 with the whole class to make sure they all know what they have to do.

> **Answers**
> 2 have been closed down.
> 3 can be used for lighting homes.
> 4 will be subsidised by the government.
> 5 is heated.
> 6 to be consumed in summer months.

❺ Although candidates often make mistakes with the passive, you can point out that students who use it correctly and appropriately will gain marks in the exam.

> **Answers**
> 2 ~~can solve~~ can be solved
> 3 ~~not all subjects teach~~ not all subjects can be taught / not all subjects are taught
> 4 ~~should reduce~~ should be reduced
> 5 ~~which caused~~ which is caused
> 6 ~~are doing~~ are done
> 7 ~~is used for~~ is used by

Unit 5 photocopiable activity: Environmental journey

Time: 40 minutes

> **Objectives**
>
> - To build confidence in giving extended responses to Speaking Part 3 questions
> - To practise the use of passive and active verbs
> - To recycle vocabulary related to *nature, the environment, tourist* and *tourism*

Before class

You will need one photocopy of the activity page on page 58 for each student and Rules on page 57 for each group of 3 or 4 students. You will also need a set of counters and one dice for each group.

In class

❶ Divide the class into groups of three or four to play the game.

❷ Explain the Rules on page 57 (you may wish to give a copy to each group).

❸ Demonstrate the game before students start to play.

- For 'Speaking Challenge' (grey squares), write the following question on the board and elicit some ideas and vocabulary students could use when answering it: *What are the most urgent environmental issues in the world today?*

- For 'Grammar Check' (white squares), write the following sentence on the board: *Governments could limit the amount of international tourism.* Ask the students to say whether the main verb is active or passive, and demonstrate how to switch it from active to passive, (*suggested answer: The amount of international tourism could be limited by governments.*)

- During the game, be ready to sort out any disagreements about the 'Grammar Check' sentences, particularly where students come up with an answer which is different from the one given in the suggested answers below, but is nevertheless correct.

Extension idea After the game, students could each choose one of the 'Speaking Challenge' questions and research it further online. This could lead to a short written project or a class presentation.

Rules

1 Work in groups of three or four to play the game.

2 Take turns to play the game. Play passes to the left. When it is your turn, roll the dice and move to the correct square.

3 If you land on a grey square (Speaking challenge), you must speak for 90 seconds about the question. If you start to run out of ideas before the time is up, the other students can help you to complete your turn by asking follow-up questions such as *What are the reasons for that?* or *Can you give us an example?*

- If you land on a white square (Grammar check), you must look carefully at the sentence and decide if the main verb is active or passive. You must then switch the verb from active to passive (or vice versa) to make a correct sentence which has the same meaning. Your teacher will be the referee if you disagree with the other students.
- If you land on a black square, follow the instructions.

4 If you land on a square which is already occupied by another player, or which has already been answered by another player, move forward one square.

5 The winner is the first person to reach the last square.

Suggested answers for 'Grammar Check' squares

3 The dolphin is considered by many people to be an endangered species.

5 Many countries use nuclear energy.

8 We use a lot of energy every day.

12 Many experts are worried nowadays by the increase in global temperatures.

16 Too many wind turbines might spoil the countryside.

19 Scientists take climate change seriously.

21 Steps must be taken by the tourism industry to preserve the countryside.

23 International tourism has created several problems.

28 Natural disasters may be caused by global warming.

32 Governments should harness renewable energy sources.

35 Emissions may be reduced by the use of electric cars.

39 Several factors influence pollution in the countryside.

41 Governments must take action to reduce global warming.

44 Many species could be saved by wildlife conservation programmes.

47 The environment is affected by tourism in various different ways.

Environmental journey

1 START	**2** What can be done to save endangered species?	**3** Many people consider the dolphin to be an endangered species.	**4** Move back one square.	**5** Nuclear energy is used in many countries.
10 Move forward two squares.	**9** Why are people worried about rising sea levels?	**8** A lot of energy is used by us every day.	**7** Has the tourism industry become too large in recent years?	**6** Miss a turn.
11 How can we reduce our dependence on fossil fuels?	**12** The increase in global temperatures worries many experts nowadays.	**13** Move back two squares.	**14** How does recycling help the environment?	**15** Miss a turn.
20 Is it important to stop the destruction of forests?	**19** Climate change is taken seriously by scientists.	**18** Move forward one square.	**17** Should the tourism industry have to pay for environmental damage?	**16** The countryside might be spoiled by too many wind turbines.
21 The tourist industry must take steps to preserve the countryside.	**22** Move back two squares.	**23** Several problems have been created by international tourism.	**24** Miss a turn.	**25** Do we use too many plastic bags?
30 Why should we protect areas of unspoilt countryside?	**29** Move back two squares.	**28** Global warming may cause natural disasters.	**27** What are the most important sources of renewable energy?	**26** Move forward one square.
31 Miss a turn.	**32** Renewable energy sources should be harnessed by governments.	**33** What can individual tourists do to protect the environment?	**34** Move forward one square.	**35** The use of electric cars may reduce emissions.
40 Miss a turn.	**39** Pollution in the countryside is influenced by several factors.	**38** Move forward two squares.	**37** How can we reduce greenhouse gas emissions?	**36** Miss a turn.
41 Action must be taken by governments to reduce global warming.	**42** In what ways can eco-tourism benefit the environment?	**43** Move back two squares.	**44** Many species can be saved by wildlife conservation programmes.	**45** Move forward one square.
50 FINISH	**49** Are individuals or governments responsible for protecting the environment?	**48** Miss a turn.	**47** Tourism affects the environment in various different ways.	**46** How can renewable energy help the environment?

Vocabulary extension
Unit 5

Abbreviations: n/pln = noun / plural noun; v = verb; adj = adjective; adv = adverb; p = phrase;
T/I = transitive/intransitive; C/U = countable/uncountable

become extinct *vp* If a type of animal or plant has become extinct, it no longer exists.

campaigner *n* [C] a person who takes part in activities which are intended to change something in society

clean energy *n* [U] clean energy comes from sources that do not cause pollution.

damage *v* to harm or break something

damage *n* [U] physical harm that has been done to something

developed country *n* [C] a rich country with a lot of industry

developing country *n* [C] a poor country with industry that is not very advanced

disaster *n* [C] something that causes a lot of harm or damage

drop litter *vp* to let pieces of rubbish fall onto the ground

emerging economy *n* [C] a country whose economy is becoming stronger and more important in the world

environmental group *n* [C] a group of people who try to protect the environment

extinction *n* [U] the situation when a type of animal or plant no longer exists

global warming *n* [U] the increase in the temperature of the air around the world

green *adj* relating to nature and protecting the environment

harm *n* [U] hurt or damage

harm *v* to hurt or damage something or someone

industrial pollution *n* [U] damage caused to water, air, etc. by harmful substances produced by industrial processes

noise pollution *n* [U] levels of noise which upset or harm people

nuclear power *n* [U] energy that is produced when the structure of the central part of an atom is changed

ocean *n* [C] one of the five main areas that the sea is divided into

ocean current *n* [C] the movement of the water in an ocean

planet *n* [C] a large, round object in space that moves around the sun or another star

polar ice caps *pln* [C] the thick layers of ice that cover areas of land at the North and South poles

pollute *v* T to make water, air, soil, etc. dirty or harmful

population increase *n* [U] when the number of people living in the world or in a particular area gets bigger

preserve *v* T to keep something the same or prevent it from being damaged or destroyed

protect the environment *p* to make sure that the environment is not harmed

rainforest *n* [C] a forest with a lot of tall trees where it rains a lot

recycle rubbish *p* to collect and treat things that have been thrown away in order to produce materials that can be used again

resource *n* [C] something that a country, person, or organisation has which they can use

smoke *n* [U] the grey or black gas that is produced when something burns

sustainable lifestyle *n* [C] a way of living that does not cause damage to the environment

the Earth *n* [U] the planet that we live on

toxic waste *n* [U] poisonous substances that are left over from things that have been used, especially in industry

traffic fumes *pln* [C] unpleasant gas or smoke that comes from vehicles

Unit 6 Making money, spending money

Unit objectives

- **Reading Section 1:** practising scanning; labelling a diagram; True / False / Not Given questions; flow-chart completion
- **Vocabulary:** verb + *to do* / verb + *doing*; words and phrases connected with finance; words and phrases connected with shops and shopping
- **Listening Section 2:** matching; labelling a diagram
- **Speaking Parts 2 and 3:** strategies for correcting oneself; re-expressing an idea and hesitating
- **Pronunciation:** word stress
- **Writing Task 2:** structuring an essay expressing advantages and disadvantages; paragraphing; writing the middle paragraphs of an essay
- **Key grammar:** relative pronouns and relative clauses

Starting off

❶ *As a warmer* Write these sentences on the board:

- *I only go shopping when I have to.*
- *Shopping is my favourite free-time activity.*
- *I quite enjoy shopping when I'm in the right mood.*

Tell students to work in small groups and to say which sentences best describe them. Ask them to give reasons and examples.

Extension idea Ask students to take turns to tell each other about their favourite shop, where it is, what it sells, how often they go there and why they like it so much. Tell them they should each speak for 1–2 minutes.

Reading   Section 1

❶

> **Answers**
> 2 f 3 c 4 d 5 e 6 g 7 a

Extension idea To give practice in scanning, ask students to scan the passage on page 58 and to underline the words from the exercise. Give two minutes for this.

❷

> **Suggested answers**
> The passage will probably be about retailers' understanding of shoppers' psychology and how they can use it to get people to buy more.

Extension idea Students may have quite a lot of ideas about supermarkets' methods.

- Ask them to work in small groups and brainstorm a list of things supermarkets do to persuade customers to buy things.
- Round up the ideas with the whole class and write them on the board.
- Practise scanning again: give students three minutes and ask them to see how many of the ideas on the board are mentioned in the passage.

Note: If you do this Extension idea, you can omit Exercise 3.

❸ *Alternative treatment* See the Extension idea in Exercise 2.

> **Suggested answers**
> Any three from the following: getting people to slow down; promoting goods near the entrance; getting people to relax and enjoy themselves; making people feel good by offering fresh fruit and vegetables early on; forcing people to walk to the back of the store to get necessary items; placing popular items halfway along aisles so shoppers have to search for them among other goods and to increase the length of time they spend in the store; encouraging feelings of hunger with smells from the bakery; placing more profitable products at eye level or slightly to the right; placing goods where they're more easily seen; offering fitting rooms and using 'decoy' items to help customers decide.

4 Labelling a diagram tests students' ability to scan to locate specific information using words on the diagram to help them. Tell students that diagram tasks always have a heading and, if students can, they should use this to scan the passage for the section where the diagram is described. (*Note*: some diagrams are described in a small section of the passage, while others are dealt with over a larger section.) Ask students to:

- check how many words they need. (Note: if the instructions say NO MORE THAN THREE WORDS, one- or two-word answers are also possible. The words/phrases will add significant meaning to the diagram, so will not be small grammar words, unless needed to complete a phrase.)

- make sure they understand the diagram and what they are being asked for before looking in the passage (hence Questions 1 and 2 here).

Extension idea Ask students to briefly say whether the layout is similar to supermarkets in their own country.

> **Answers**
> **1** the layout of a typical supermarket
> **2** Gaps 1 and 2 explain the purpose of the zones; gap 3 is a type of counter; gap 4 is probably an object or type of product.

5 Tell students that underlining words will help make sure that they actually use words from the passage to label the diagram.

- Students should also underline words on the diagram around the gaps. These will help them to locate the information they need in the passage; phrases like *chill zone* and *decompression zone* in inverted commas are clearly quoted directly from the passage, so students should scan directly for those and then read that part of the passage carefully.

- Keep reminding students that they can lose a lot of marks by not copying the words exactly and by not spelling them correctly.

> **Answers**
> **1** promotion   **2** unplanned purchases
> **3** fruit and vegetables   **4** popular items

6 This is the third time students have worked on the True / False / Not Given task in this course.

- Elicit that students should not read the whole passage again carefully. (*Suggested underlining*: 6 fruit and vegetables 7 In-store bakeries 8 right-handed people easier to persuade 9 leaving ... without buying 10 'decoy' items)

- Give students a time limit, say three minutes, to locate the parts of the passage which deal with each question. Point out that they will find the answers in the same order in the passage as the questions, so there should be no need to go back and re-scan a part of the passage more than once to locate the relevant sections.

- The task in this unit concentrates on the difference between FALSE and NOT GIVEN, which often confuses students.

- Elicit that students should choose FALSE when the passage contradicts the statement and NOT GIVEN when there is nothing in the passage which states the information in the question. If there are any doubts, elicit the meaning of 'contradicts'.

- When students have finished, they should compare their answers with a partner. Encourage them to quote from the passage to justify their answers. This will encourage them to base their answers on evidence rather than supposition.

> **Answers**
> **5** NOT GIVEN (The greeters are mentioned, but it doesn't say whether they increase sales or not.)
> **6** TRUE (*Fruit and vegetables can be easily damaged, so they should be bought at the end ... selecting these items makes people feel good, so they feel less guilty about reaching for less healthy food later on.*)
> **7** NOT GIVEN (The passage says *central bakeries are ... much more efficient* – but it doesn't say anything about the range of products.)
> **8** NOT GIVEN (The passage says *To be on the right-hand-side of an eye-level selection is often considered the very best place, because most people are right-handed*, but it doesn't say they are more easily persuaded.)
> **9** FALSE (*People say they leave shops empty-handed more often because they are 'unable to decide' than because prices are too high ...*)
> **10** FALSE (*In order to avoid a situation where a customer decides not to buy either product, a third 'decoy' item, which is not quite as good as the other two, is placed beside them to make the choice easier and more pleasurable.*)

7 Like labelling a diagram, flow-chart completion tests students' ability to scan to locate specific information using words on the chart to help them.

- Tell students it is important to read the title of the chart: this will help them to understand it and to locate the section of the passage which deals with it.

- Ask students to work in pairs to write a sentence which expresses what the chart shows, using their own words. Round up with the whole class, discussing which the best 'paraphrase' is. Students can vote to decide which sentence is the winner.

> **Suggested answer**
> The flow chart shows the process of producing bread inside supermarkets.

❽ Elicit that students should:

- check how many words they need for each gap.

- copy words exactly from the passage.

- read their answers afterwards to check they make sense, reflect what they have understood, and are grammatically correct.

> **Answers**
> **11** frozen ingredients   **12** appetites
> **13** ready meals

You can point out that, in dealing with this Reading passage, students have not had to read it carefully in detail from beginning to end. They should realise that the way they read the passage is determined by the type of tasks they have to deal with, and these tasks should be dealt with in ways which are the most efficient to get the correct answers in the time available.

Listening   Section 2

❶ *As a warmer* Ask students to work in small groups with books closed.

- They should brainstorm as many words and phrases connected with banks as they can in three minutes.

- Round up with the whole class and write useful vocabulary on the board. Ask students to explain words and phrases they have suggested which other students don't know.

Follow up with Exercise 1.

> **Answers**
> **2** c   **3** g   **4** a   **5** e   **6** d   **7** h   **8** f

❷ Explain to students that they will always hear the answers in the same order as the questions.

Mention that they will sometimes have to underline the whole question when underlining the key idea.

> **Suggested answers**
> **1** branch on the campus
> **2** free gift for new customers
> **3** special interest rates for students
> **4** no bank charges for certain customers

Extension idea 1 Tell students that what they hear on the recording will have a slightly different wording from the questions. So when they prepare, it is a good idea to rephrase the questions in their own words and/or think about different ways in which the speaker might express the same idea. Ask them to work in pairs and explain what each question means. To get them started, you can elicit the first one from the whole class. (*Suggested answers*: 1 the bank has an office inside the university 2 you get a present when you become a client 3 students pay a lower percentage on their loans 4 some clients do not have to pay the bank for its services.)

Extension idea 2 With weaker classes, write the suggested answers from Extension idea 1 on the board in a different order. Ask students to match them to the questions. Elicit what words in the suggested answers correspond with words in the questions (e.g. *gift = present*).

To make sure they have understood the instructions, ask: *Do you need to use all the banks in your answers?* (*Answer*: no, just four)

❸

> **Answers**
> **1** B   **2** D   **3** C   **4** E

❹ Labelling a diagram tests similar listening skills to labelling a map, which students have seen in Unit 2.

- Before listening, students should orientate themselves on the diagram.

- Students should look at the words around the gaps, as these will help them to hear the word(s) they need.

- They should also look at other information which is given (in this case, for example, the cardholder's name) as this is intended to make sure they don't get lost during the exercise. To reinforce this point, you can elicit the information already on the diagram.

Extension idea Make sure students know phrases like: *at the top, halfway down, on the left, in the bottom right-hand corner*. You can teach these by asking where things are on the diagram, or in another picture in the book.

❺

> **Answers**
> **5** picture   **6** magnetic strip   **7** signature
> **8** bank logo   **9** date   **10** chip

Extension idea Round up with the whole class by asking how the answers are spelled. If there is any disagreement about spelling, write the different suggestions on the board and ask the class to choose the correct one.

❻ *Alternative treatment* Write the following topics on the board:

- *friendly staff*
- *close to home*
- *nice offices*
- *quick service*
- *low interest rates*
- *easy to get a loan*

Ask students to work in groups and put the topics in order of importance when choosing a bank. Ask: *Is there anything else you would add?*

Vocabulary
Verb + *to do* / verb + *doing*

❶ Tell students they will have to learn these verbs individually and elicit that the negative of *to do* is *not to do* and the negative of *doing* is *not doing*.

> **Answers**
> **2** to sell; to be   **3** browsing
> **4** to purchase   **5** not buying   **6** not to buy

Go through the Language reference on page 105. Suggest that students keep the lists of verbs handy and to use them when doing Writing tasks. In this way, they will learn to use them correctly.

❷ Students can refer to the Language reference on page 105 when doing this exercise and Exercise 3.

> **Answers**
> **2** ✓   **3** to improve improving   **4** buying to buy
> **5** ✓   **6** increasing to increase   **7** buying to buy
> **8** to shop shopping

❸

> **Answers**
> **2** to go   **3** watching   **4** to improve   **5** having
> **6** to come   **7** buying   **8** to get

❹ *Alternative treatment* If your students have little experience of supermarkets, ask them to talk about other types of shopping that they know well.

Speaking   Parts 2 and 3

❶ *As a warmer 1* With books closed, ask students:

- *What are your favourite advertisements on TV?*
- *Have you ever bought anything as a result of an advertisement?*

As a warmer 2 With books open, ask students to look at the images. Ask where they might see each of the ads and what they are advertising.

Note: At this stage, students should only make notes, not actually do the task. They will do that later.

Alternative treatment If students are short of ideas, ask them to work in small groups and think of some advertisements they found persuasive first.

❷ 🎧

> **Answers**
> **what the advertisement was for:** *energy drink – sporting activity*
> **where you saw or read it:** *television*
> **what the advertisement consisted of:** *Olympic athlete – 100 metres – natural ingredients*
> **why you found it so persuasive:** *famous successful person, university exams, school volleyball team*

Alternative treatment Write this checklist on the board (similar to the one from Unit 2) and ask students to assess Irina's performance when they listen. They can listen twice if necessary.

Does she …

… start answering the points on the prompt card straight away?

… deal with all the points on the prompt card?

… keep to the topic on the card?

… keep speaking for the time allowed?

… sound interested in what she's saying?

Note: This is a good moment to do the Pronunciation tasks on word stress, which are based on Irina's answer.

❸ If students have done the pronunciation section, ask them to choose four or five words from Pronunciation Exercise 2 to use when they give their talk.

Extension idea Photocopy, cut out and give students either Card A or Card B below. Students:

- first work alone to prepare and make notes (give one minute for this).
- then work in pairs and take turns to give their talks (give 1–2 minutes each).

❹ *Alternative treatment* Give students the photocopiable Word list on page 69 of this book and ask them to look for vocabulary they can use when answering.

❺ 🎧

> **Answers**
> **Reasons:** to know a new product exists; to give information about products; to attract new customers
> **Examples:** clothes; new drink for sportspeople

6 🎧 Students need strategies to help them deal with things like forgetting a word or phrase. Paraphrasing is dealt with in Unit 7, but point out here how Irina avoids a breakdown in her speech by using a simple phrase: *what's the word*. These strategies can help increase scores in the test.

> **Answers**
> **1** in other words   **2** I mean
> **3** how do you say / what's the word

7 Students should change partners for this exercise.

> ***Extension idea*** Photocopy, cut out, and give students Cards C and D below.
>
> - Ask students to change partners. They then take turns to be the 'examiner'.
> - The 'examiner' should read the questions. Their partners should answer them.
> - When they have finished, students change roles.

A

Describe an interesting shopping trip you once made.

You should say:

- where you went
- why you went there
- what you bought

and explain why the trip was so interesting.

B

Describe something you bought recently which has been very useful to you.

You should say:

- what it is
- why you bought it
- where you bought it

and explain how it has been so useful to you.

C

To shop or not to shop?

- Why do you think people spend so much of their free time shopping?
- Why do some people prefer to save money instead of spending it?
- How do you think parents can teach children to manage their money well?

D

Big versus small shops

- How has shopping changed in recent years?
- When is it better to visit small specialist shops rather than large stores?
- What can small shops do to attract more customers?

Pronunciation
Word stress

1 🎧 You can mention that one of the main reasons why people do not understand when someone speaks to them is when the stress is placed on the wrong part of the word. As an example, say *actually* to your students three times, each time placing the stress on a different syllable. Ask them which pronunciation is correct and why.

> **Answer**
> 'actually

2

> **Answers**
> **1** advertisements (4)   **2** persuasive (3)   **3** energy (3)
> **4** activity (4)   **5** television (4)   **6** generally (3)
> **7** advertising (4)   **8** usually (3)   **9** product (2)
> **10** person (2)   **11** famous (2)   **12** successful (3)
> **13** university (5)   **14** expensive (3)   **15** energetic (4)

3 🎧 Tell students there are no clear rules for where stress is placed in words.

> **Answers**
> **1** ad'vertisements   **2** per'suasive   **3** 'energy
> **4** ac'tivity   **5** 'television   **6** 'generally
> **7** 'advertising   **8** 'usually   **9** 'product
> **10** 'person   **11** 'famous   **12** suc'cessful
> **13** uni'versity   **14** ex'pensive   **15** ener'getic

4

> **Answers**
> **1** The stress is on different syllables in the related words (*ad'vertisements, 'advertising; 'energy, ener'getic*).
> **2** the final syllable

Extension idea Show students how a good learner's dictionary indicates word stress.

5 ***Extension idea*** Ask students to pick four or five words from Exercise 2 which they have problems with, and to use them in sentences. Their partners should listen and say whether they have placed the stress correctly.

Writing Task 2

1 *As a warmer* With books closed, ask students:

- *Have you ever bought anything over the Internet? Why? Why not?*

Follow up with questions such as:

- *What did you buy? Why?*
- *Did you have any problems buying over the Internet?*
- *Are there any things you would never buy over the Internet?*

When students have finished the exercise in the book:

- ask them to change partners and compare lists.
- ask them to decide which are the two most important advantages and the two most important disadvantages.
- then round up ideas with the whole class.

2 Remind students that in order to achieve above Band 5, they must organise their answer logically and use paragraphs. Each paragraph should have a clear purpose and address a different aspect of the subject.

Ask students to compare their ideas in pairs and give reasons. Ask them to say what the purpose of each paragraph is.

> **Answers**
> *... outweighs any drawbacks. //*
> (general introduction and writer's opinion)
>
> *There are two main ... you do not really want. //*
> (the main disadvantages of buying over the Internet)
>
> *On the other hand, shopping ... are often cheaper. //*
> (advantages)
>
> *All in all, I think ...*
> (summary, expressing writer's opinion exactly)

3

> **Answers**
> **1, 2** students' own answers
> **3** They are an introduction to the subject of the paragraph.

4 Students look at the sample answer and record any useful words or phrases.

5 *Alternative treatment* To get weaker classes started, you may have to elicit an advantage and a disadvantage. (*Suggested answers*: Advantages: more independent; make their own decisions; may make more money if their business is successful; can work when and where they want; have more control over their future. Disadvantages: may have to work much harder; there may be more risk; may need financial help to get started; may lose money)

6 Tell students that if they are not sure how to start a paragraph, their first sentence can say what the purpose of the paragraph is.

- Elicit what the purposes will be of paragraphs 2 and 3 that they work on here.
- Tell students they should use ideas they thought of when doing Exercise 5 to complete the paragraphs.

Extension idea 1 Ask students to suggest other opening sentences for paragraphs which state the purpose of the paragraph. Give them some examples.

- *Some people think that starting their own business is too risky. On the one hand, they say that ...*
- *However, not everyone agrees with this. Some people prefer to work for themselves because ...*
- *There are advantages and disadvantages in running your own business. One advantage is that ...*
- *Similarly, working for a company has its pros and cons. People who do this ...*

Extension idea 2 If your classroom is equipped with networked computers and an interactive whiteboard, you can project students' paragraphs for the whole class to see and comment on. You can also work on correcting errors together.

7 When students have finished, ask them to join with another pair and compare their ideas and their plans. Ask them to be ready to change their plans in reaction to any good ideas they get from the other pair.

8 This task is probably best done for homework. In this case, tell students to give themselves 40 minutes to complete the task, as they would have in the exam, and to be strict about the timing.

Sample answer

It has become more and more popular for students to work for a period of time rather than going straight to university. There are advantages to this, but I feel that it is also a risk and could lead to some problems.

One of the obvious disadvantages of getting a job is that you may find that you cannot get a university place at a later stage. This is because there may be a lot of competition for places, and the longer you wait, the harder it may be to get one. You could even find that the course you want has been changed or dropped.

Another disadvantage is that you can lose the habit of studying. For example, school students are trained to use a range of study skills, which help them achieve academic success. However, if you are not using these skills regularly, it is easy to forget them. This could make university life much harder.

On the other hand, there are several advantages to getting a job. The first is that you can become independent. For example, people who earn their own money can afford to rent their own apartment. In addition, some of the money can be saved and used to pay for university fees. Another advantage is that working gives you some time to think about what you would really like to study. This is very useful if you are unsure about your future career.

Overall, I think there are arguments for and against the idea of working between school and university. The important thing is to be aware of these issues and choose the path that best suits your personal situation.

(277 words)

Key grammar
Relative pronouns and relative clauses

❶ Like other grammar areas included in this course, this is intended as revision and a reminder. Students will achieve a higher Band score in the Writing paper by writing more complex sentences, for example, using relative clauses.

When they have finished this brief first exercise, go through the Language reference on page 105 with them.

> **Answers**
> **2** which   **3** that   **4** what

❷ Tell students to look out for these types of mistakes when using relative clauses.

> **Answers**
> **2** ~~who~~ which/that   **3** ~~where~~ which/that
> **4** ~~who they are~~ who/that are   **5** ~~who~~ which/that
> **6** ~~what~~ which/that

❸

> **Answers**
> **2** what   **3** which/that; what   **4** who/that
> **5** What; which/that

Vocabulary and grammar review
Unit 5
Answers
Vocabulary

❶ **2** greenhouse   **3** climate   **4** levels   **5** fossil
6 renewable   **7** emissions   **8** endangered

❷ **2** the environment   **3** Tourism; tourists   **4** nature

Grammar

❸ *Suggested answer*

Could asphalt and concrete eventually be replaced by solar panels?

These days, **solar panels can be found** just about everywhere. **It has been suggested** that if **a gigantic number of solar panels were laid down** over a wide area, **enough sunlight could be absorbed** to power entire cities, effectively ending our energy crisis. The problem is that **the countryside would be spoilt** if **large areas of it were covered** with these things. On the other hand, there is a network of roads all over the country, and now **even cars are being manufactured** with solar panels on them. If **the two are put together**, you get a unique solution: solar panels on our highways. This could mean that **the panels could be placed** along roadways as sound barriers, or an even more extreme idea – that **the roads themselves will be made** out of solar panels.

Vocabulary and grammar review
Unit 6

Answers

Vocabulary

❶ **2** employing; offering   **3** to buy; not to do   **4** to save
5 working   **6** playing   **7** to save; to take out   **8** to be

❷

I	G	O	O	D	L	U	S	C	E	T	K
N	W	I	T	H	I	A	E	C	L	N	T
T	S	T	Q	I	V	K	N	M	K	U	T
E	M	T	L	I	N	A	L	L	O	P
R	R	M	N	N	L	C	F	D	Y	C	L
E	K	G	F	A	Y	L	R	V	R	C	R
S	S	M	B	R	Q	W	R	E	X	A	V
T	V	T	P	T	W	K	Z	Z	D	C	P
R	D	I	R	E	C	T	D	E	B	I	T
A	V	M	R	M	K	N	M	R	R	Y	T
T	G	O	V	E	R	D	R	A	F	T	H
E	D	C	L	B	R	A	N	C	H	J	W

The hidden message is: Good luck with IELTS

Grammar

❸ **2** what   **3** why   **4** What   **5** where   **6** who/that
7 whose/where   **8** which/that

❹ **2** The reason why students often leave their jobs is that they take up too much time.
3 Young people whose parents are ambitious for them are often in a hurry to go to university.
4 Students often take a part-time job which/that helps pay their university fees.
5 Students who work often find this distracts them from their studies.
OR Students work, which they find often distracts them from their studies.
6 Students often find it difficult to find a job near the college where they study.
7 I got my first job at the age of 18 when I left school.
OR I left school at the age of 18 when I got my first job.
8 I got my first job in the town where my cousin lives.

Unit 6 photocopiable activity: Supermarket revolution

Time: 40-50 minutes

Objectives

- To practise spoken fluency in a presentation
- To revise strategies for correcting oneself; re-expressing an idea and hesitating
- To revise verb + *to do* / verb + *doing*
- To recycle vocabulary related to shopping

Before class

You need one copy of the activity page on page 68 for each student.

In class

❶ Students work in pairs to do exercise 1, which revises verb patterns with infinitive and -*ing* forms.

Answers
a to persuade   **b** to be   **c** going   **d** to buy
e to give   **f** buying   **g** to look   **h** (to) remember

❷ Divide the class into groups of three. Explain that they are going to prepare and deliver a pitch (try to sell their idea) for a new type of supermarket. Go through the instructions to exercise 2 on the activity page.

❸ Hand out a set of student's role cards to each group. Ask the groups to allocate one of the individual roles to each member. Tell them that they will give a short presentation to the class.

- Allow at least 10 minutes for students to prepare notes.

- Monitor for errors which you can address at the end of the class. Pay special attention to the use of relative clauses, infinitive or -*ing* forms, word stress, and vocabulary.

- Before the students give their presentations, remind students of phrases for correcting oneself or for re-expressing an idea and hesitating (e.g. *I mean*; *what's the word*).

- Each group gives their presentation. Allow the other students to ask the questions they have prepared.

- Conduct a class vote to see which group should receive the funding for the project.

- Round up with a feedback session. Be sure to give positive feedback about the presentations, before writing errors on the board for students to correct.

Supermarket revolution

❶ Complete these sentences with the correct form of the verb in brackets. Then talk to a partner about how similar they are to your own experience of supermarket shopping

a Supermarkets try too hard .... (persuade) customers to buy things they don't need.

b In my experience, supermarkets tend .... (be) badly organised so that it's hard to find what I need.

c I have to say that I don't really enjoy .... (go) shopping and prefer to buy everything online.

d Shopping at a big supermarket enables me .... (buy) everything I need on one weekly trip.

e I think modern shoppers expect supermarkets .... (give) them perfect service, which doesn't exist.

f When I go to the supermarket I often end up .... (buy) something I didn't originally intend to buy.

g Busy people like me never bother .... (look) for bargains, because we don't have time.

h I usually need a shopping list to help me .... (remember) everything I need.

❷ Work in small groups. You have decided to start a new supermarket business to meet the needs of today's customers. You can use an idea of your own, or one of these.

- a supermarket which only sells **local products** (produced within 20km of the shop).

- a **community supermarket** staffed entirely by unpaid workers who live nearby and who will receive a 20% discount on all products.

- a '**2 in 1**' supermarket which not only sells products but also works as a bank.

- a **virtual** supermarket which only exists online and cannot be visited by customers in person.

❸ Your teacher will give each of you a card with further instructions.

- -

Students' role cards

Speaker 1	Speaker 2	Speaker 3
You are responsible for choosing the product range.	You are responsible for advertising and promotions.	You are responsible for the organisation of the supermarket.
Make sure you mention the following points, giving reasons and examples.	Make sure you mention the following points, giving reasons and examples.	Make sure you mention the following points, giving reasons and examples.
• whether you will sell own-label or branded products • whether you will concentrate on luxury or value products, or a mix of both • where your products will come from (local or international producers)	• how you can persuade your existing customers to buy more • what special bargains you can offer • how you will advertise the supermarket to attract new customers	(If you are an online supermarket, talk about the design of the website.) • how customers will be greeted • how customers can interact with you • whether you will have any special features inside the shop

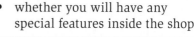

Vocabulary extension
Unit 6

Abbreviations: n/pln = noun / plural noun; v = verb; adj = adjective; adv = adverb; p = phrase; T/I = transitive/intransitive; C/U = countable/uncountable

borrow money *vp* to get money from a person or an organisation such as a bank with the intention of paying it back

charge *n* [C] the amount of money that you have to pay for something, especially for an activity or a service

charge *v* to ask someone to pay an amount of money for something, especially for an activity or a service

client *n* [C] someone who pays someone else for services or advice

consumer *n* [C] someone who buys or uses goods or services

currency *n* [C] the units of money used in a particular country

customer *n* [C] a person or organisation that buys goods or services from a shop or business

discount *n* [C] a reduction in price

exchange rate *n* [C] the amount of one country's money that you can buy with a particular amount of another country's money

goods *pln* [U] items which are made to be sold

insurance *n* [U] an agreement in which you pay a company money and they pay your costs if something you own is lost, stolen or broken, or if you have an accident, injury, etc.

interest rate *n* [U] the percent of an amount of money which is charged by a bank or other financial company when you borrow money, or paid by them when you keep money in an account

invest money *vp* to use your money to buy something such as shares or property with the aim of making a profit from it

investment *n* [C] money that is used to buy something with the aim of making a profit

lend money *vp* to give someone money with an agreement that they will pay it back at a later date

lose money *vp* If a person or a business is losing money, it is spending more money than it is receiving.

pay money in *vp* to put money into a bank account

receive a pension *vp* to be paid a regular sum of money after you have stopped working

make a loan *vp* to give someone money with an agreement that they will pay it back at a later date

make a profit *vp* to make more money from selling goods or services than it costs to produce or obtain them

rent a flat *vp* If you rent a flat to someone, you let them live there in return for money, and if you rent a flat from someone, you pay them money to live there.

retirement *n* [U] the period of your life after you have stopped working

receive a salary *vp* to be paid a fixed amount of money each month for the work that you do

sales *pln* the number of items sold

save money *vp* to keep money rather than spending it

supermarket chain *n* [C] a group of supermarkets in different places that are all owned by the same company

supplier *n* [C] a person, company or country that sells a product or a service

pay tax *p* to pay an amount of money to the government, for example a part of the money you earn

taxpayer *n* [C] a person who pays tax

valuable *adj* Valuable objects could be sold for a lot of money.

good value *n* [U] If something is good value, it is of good quality or there is a lot of it so it is worth the amount of money is costs.

withdraw cash *p* to take out money from a bank

worth *adj* If something is worth a particular amount of money, that is its value.

❶ Complete the sentences by writing a word in each space.

0   Someone who does not eat meat is a ...*vegetarian*...

1   Scientists have created .... power by capturing heat from the sun.

2   Burning fossil fuels, such as oil and gas, pollutes the ....

3   As a result of hunting, some animal species have now become ....

4   Cutting down forests not only adds to global warming but also destroys animal ....

5   Some forms of .... energy are unreliable because they depend on the weather.

❷ Choose the best alternative (A, B or C) for each of the sentences.

0   Petrol-driven vehicles ....*A*........ dangerous quantities of greenhouse gases.
   A emit   **B** leave   **C** pump

1   Conservationists agree that we need to do more to .... rare animal species.
   A guard   **B** protect   **C** defend

2   If more people .... to alternative power sources, the air would become cleaner.
   A moved   **B** exchanged   **C** switched

3   Some factories .... toxic fumes into the atmosphere.
   A release   **B** put   **C** deliver

4   Most pollution problems were .... by human beings.
   A formed   **B** shaped   **C** created

5   The area where I live is surrounded .... forest.
   A of   **B** by   **C** over

6   It can be very expensive to .... electricity using wind or tidal power.
   A raise   **B** make   **C** produce

❸ Complete the sentences with the correct form of the words in brackets.

0   Many supermarkets now have a ......*bakery*...... (bake) in the store.

1   Unfortunately, small .... (retail) have to charge more for their products than large superstores.

2   If you cannot find what you are looking for, you should ask an .... (assist) for help.

3   Some customers believe that there is too much .... (choose) in shops today.

4   Psychologists have many ideas that can help shopkeepers increase their .... (sell).

5   During the bad weather, the supermarket .... (shelf) were empty.

❹ Put statements a–g in the correct order to describe how an avalanche happens.

a   When the wind blows, the top layer moves slightly forward and hangs over the edge of the mountain.

b   In the first stage, a very cold layer of snow falls on the mountain.

c   An avalanche happens when a lot of snow falls down a mountainside.

d   As a consequence, when someone makes a loud noise or skis over the snow, the layer can become loose.

e   Next, a top layer of snow forms that is wetter and heavier.

f   Then it breaks away from the bottom layer and slides down the mountainside.

1 ......*C*......   2 ....   3 ....   4 ....   5 ....   6 ....

❺ Complete the sentences by writing the verb in brackets in the correct form: active or passive.

0   Generally, about 5,000 wind turbines ...are..needed. (need) to replace one coal-fired power station.

1   During the world's worst tropical storm, wind speeds .... (reach) over 310 kilometres per hour.

2   The Internet .... (can use) to find out about the weather.

3   In the past, most wildfires .... (cause) by lightning strikes.

4   Basically, this solar panel .... (consist) of black water pipes inside a glass box.

5   When the storm hit the area, hot air .... (blow) across the desert by the strong winds.

6   Energy resources .... (fit) into two broad types: renewable and non-renewable.

❻ Choose the correct option in each of the sentences.

0   When I moved to Paris, I ~~started~~/opened a new bank account.

1   Most large banks have *branches/departments* in other countries.

2   As my course was expensive, I had to *get/borrow* a loan from my father.

3   When you choose a bank, it is important to make sure they offer a good *interest/savings* rate.

4   It can be very worrying to find that your bank *balance/credit* is empty.

5   Unfortunately, some banks are not willing to *give/pay* their customers an overdraft.

6   It is easy to get into *debt/debit* if you spend too much money.

❼ Complete the paragraph with words from the box. Add commas if necessary.

who	what	where	which	when	why	who

who
Everyone knows that retailers, ^ rely on their sales, have to use advertising to promote their

products. Unfortunately, as consumers, we have no choice over we see these advertisements or

they are placed. No matter we are doing, there seem to be advertisements everywhere.

They often occur on television in the middle of an important scene. Suddenly, your

concentration is interrupted by someone is trying to sell you car insurance. When this happens

on my television, the volume also increases really annoys me. I cannot understand this

happens!

Unit 7 Relationships

Starting off

❶ *As a warmer* Write these questions on the board. Then ask students to discuss them in small groups.

What do you do when you're feeling…?

… bored

… anxious

… angry

When students open their books, ask them first to look at the photos (but not the questions) and say what they think is happening in each photo. Round up with the whole class and ask students to do the exercises in the book.

Listening   Section 3

❶ Before students start, make sure they know what *project work* means. (*Answer*: a study of a particular subject done over a period of time, especially by students.) Elicit from the class examples of projects they have worked on at school. Ask: *Which ones sound the most interesting?*

Suggested answers
Students share ideas and learn from each other; students take various roles in the project so more information can be gathered and relevant topics can be covered in more depth; students have different skills/abilities to contribute to a project, so a wider range of areas can be tackled.

❷ *Alternative treatment* Ask students to look quickly at Questions 1–10. Ask:

- *How many tasks are there?* (*Answer*: two)
- *How many questions are there in each task?* (*Answer*: five) Tell students to underline any word limits (*Students should underline*: NO MORE THAN TWO in Questions 6–10). Elicit why it is important to check the listening tasks quickly when they start each listening section (*answer*: so they know what to expect when they start listening).

Suggested answers
2 What point / Victor make / Fumiko's tutor
3 What has Fumiko / already read
4 Fumiko's project must include
5 Victor / Fumiko arrange

Ask students to look at the exercise in the book. Tell them that the signals guide them through the listening and help them keep their place (e.g. they are not listening for Question 2 when Question 5 is being answered). Point out that underlining the key idea in each question before they start listening should alert them to a signal when it comes.

❸

Answers
a 2 **b** 1 **c** 4 **d** 5 **e** 3

❹ Tell students that, as they are near the end of the course, they will do the whole listening exercise (i.e. Questions 1–10) and they will hear the piece just once.

- Students have already underlined key ideas for Questions 1–5. Tell them there will be a pause between Questions 5 and 6.
- Elicit what they should do during the pause. (*Answer*: look at the title of the flow chart and underline the key ideas in the chart.)

- Tell students there are also signals in the recording which will help them listen for the right information in the flow chart. This is one reason why it is important to underline key ideas here.

5 After listening, students can compare their answers in pairs and you can then round up with the whole class. Play the recording a second time after this for students to check their answers.

> **Answers**
> 1 C   2 A   3 C   4 B   5 A
>
> 6 key terms   7 animal world
> 8 contexts   9 stages   10 influences

6

> **Answers**
> 6 first   7 that   8 that's   9 next   10 end

Extension idea When students have finished, ask how these signals are different from the signals in Exercise 3 and why. (*Answer*: They mark a <u>sequence of events</u>, because the task is a flow diagram, i.e. it describes a process stage-by-stage.)

7 You can give students practice of Speaking Part 2 with this activity.

- Give students a minute to prepare and write notes.
- Ask the student who is listening to keep track of the time and to say 'thank you' when two minutes have passed.
- Tell the student speaking to continue until their partner tells them to stop.

Vocabulary
age(s) / aged / age group

1 *As a warmer*

- Write these sentences on the board and ask students which is not correct. (*Answer*: 2)

1 *She is 18 years old.*

2 *She has 18 years.*

3 *She learned to drive aged 18.*

4 *She learned to drive at the age of 18.*

- Ask students to work in groups and compare the ages when they did the following things (you can write these on the board): *learned to swim, started learning English, met your best friend, got your first mobile phone.* Omit or replace any of these suggestions if they are not suitable for your class.
- Ask them to use correct sentences like the ones on the board to answer.
- When they have finished, round up by asking questions such as: *Who was the youngest when they learned to swim?* Students should answer with

a complete sentence (e.g. *Karim was the youngest, because he learnt to swim aged two.*). Insist on accuracy when you round up like this.

> **Answers**
> 2 age group   3 aged   4 age group   5 the age

2 Tell students there are often charts and graphs in Writing Task 1 which refer to people's ages, so it is very important to be able to use these phrases correctly. Students will have a further opportunity to activate this vocabulary in the Writing section later in this unit.

> **Answers**
> 2 between the ages of/aged between
> 3 aged 10–20 months/aged between 10 and 12 months
> 4 age group   5 in the 5 to 11 age group
> 6 group aged

Extension idea 1 If your class are mixed nationalities, ask them to think of a few questions for people of other nationalities about the education system in their countries. They could find out things like:

- the age children start school.
- the age children start learning to read.
- the age children start secondary school.
- the earliest age young people can leave school.
- the age most young people finish university.

Students then circulate round the class and ask questions. When they have finished, they work with a partner and report what they've found out using language they've just studied.

Extension idea 2 If your students are all the same nationality, ask them to work in pairs and imagine they are going to give information to someone from another country about their education system and the ages young people do things. You can suggest: *The age children start secondary school.* Students can think of other information.

They then work together and write four or five sentences using the language they have just studied. When they have finished, they compare their information with other pairs. They then discuss any differences.

Reading   Section 2

1 *As a warmer* With books closed, ask students to work in pairs and imagine that a friend of theirs is going to do the IELTS test and wants to know what the Reading Paper consists of. Ask them to think what information they can give about timing, the number of sections, the number of questions, etc. When they have finished, ask them to compare their ideas with another pair.

❷ Extension idea Ask students to read the passage quickly in three minutes and to find answers to Question 3. They then discuss their answers to the question in pairs.

❸ Before they do the tasks, ask students:

- *How many tasks are there? (Answer:* three)

- *How many questions are there in each task? (Answer:* 6, 4 and 3)

- *Are there any word limits? (Answer:* one word only for Questions 11–13)

- *What approach should you use with the first task? (Answer*: read the headings carefully first, underlining the key ideas)

It is a good idea at this stage to make students think about timing. Ask: *How long do you think you should spend on each task, bearing in mind you have 20 minutes for the whole section? (Suggested answer:* first task 12 minutes; second task four minutes; third task four minutes)

Alternative treatment Ask students to work alone and do Questions 1–6 (paragraph headings) first.

- Before they start, elicit that they should read each paragraph quickly, looking for a theme or global idea. Point out that this is often, but not always, in the first or last sentence of the paragraph.

- Give students a time limit for this activity, e.g. 10 minutes.

- When they have finished, ask students to compare their answers in pairs. You then round up with the whole class. Remind students that there are always up to three more headings than they need.

- Elicit how students should approach Questions 7–10 (matching features): underline the key ideas

in the questions, skim/scan the passage quickly to locate the experiments, read those parts of the passage carefully and choose their answers.

- Give students five minutes for this task. Then ask them to compare answers in pairs before rounding up with the whole class. Refer students to the rubric 'You may use any letter more than once' and remind them that sometimes they need to do this. At other times, there may be more options in the box than they need.

- Elicit how students should approach Questions 11–13 (sentence completion): underline the main idea in each question, scan the passage to locate the relevant part, read carefully and copy the word you need for each answer. Remind students that many candidates lose marks by not copying words correctly from the passage to the answer sheet.

- Give students five minutes for this task.

Note: You may wish to do Exercise 4 before asking students to check their answers to Questions 11–13.

❹ Tell students that avoiding these careless mistakes is the easiest way to raise their band score.

Q	Answer	Reason it was marked wrong
11	body language	two words / a noun / wrong answer
11	nervously	wrong part of speech
12	their feelings	right idea, but doesn't fit grammatically / spelling is wrong
12	themsleves	right idea, but doesn't fit grammatically / spelling is wrong
12	feeling	should be plural
13	real clues	wrong answer / two words
13	use	wrong answer (even though close to correct word)

❺ Ask students to give examples from their personal experience.

Extension idea Ask students to do the experiment described in paragraph C of the Reading passage.

- Students first work alone and think of two films, one of which is their favourite. Tell them they will have two minutes in total to explain why each of the films is their favourite (obviously in one instance, they will be lying).

- Students then work in pairs and take turns to talk about their favourite films. Their partner must listen and decide which film they are lying about.

- Students finally round up in groups by saying what signs helped them to detect when their partners were lying (if they managed to do so).

- This activity will also give them practice in speaking at length as required in Speaking Part 2.

Speaking   Part 1

❶ **As a warmer** With books closed, tell students they are going to work on Part 1 of the Speaking test. Tell them that students often get nervous before doing the Speaking test. Ask: *What can you do to deal with pre-test nerves?* Students work in groups and suggest remedies. You can suggest or elicit the following:

- Remember to take your identification (usually a passport or identity card).

- Arrive for the test with plenty of time so you're not nervous about arriving late.

- Sleep (don't study) the night before.

- Don't drink too much coffee.

- Speak in English to another candidate before doing the speaking test so that you're not speaking

English for the first time that day when you go into the test.

- Make sure you know exactly what you'll have to do before you go into the test.

- Breathe deeply.

You can also tell students what will happen when they enter the examination room (before Part 1 starts). For example, the examiner will greet them and ask them to sit down. He or she will ask them their name and where they come from, and check their identification.

Students then do the exercise in the book.

> **Answers**
> **2** familiar   **3** three   **4** vocabulary   **5** word
> **6** question

❷ Introduce the exercise by telling students that you are going to look at different ways of beginning an answer.

- Explain that they sometimes need to think a little about their reply but should try to avoid saying *um* and/or hesitating frequently. These exercises illustrate how certain opening phrases can help with this, and so improve a speaker's fluency.

- Play the recording twice before students discuss.

- Point out that some questions don't need openers because students don't need time to think of the answer, or the answer comes very readily. E.g.

– *Where do you live?*

– *I live in Kuala Lumpur.*

> **Answers**
> **1** *Um, 'make new friends', um maybe … new friends …*
> *Mmm, I'm not sure, I've never thought about that …*
> **2** The second speaker. She avoids hesitating and repeating herself. She also answers the question clearly.
> **3** It allows her time to think about her answer, while still producing accurate, clear language.

❸

> **Answers**
> **2** a   **3** e   **4** b   **5** d

Extension idea 1 Explain that openers are helpful when questions require a little thought. Ask students to work in pairs and think of one more opener they could use like the ones in the exercise. Then round up ideas with the whole class and write valid openers on the board. Elicit from students what the openers they have suggested mean, or when they can be used.

Extension idea 2 Ask students to work in pairs, choose three of the openers and then think of three complete sentences using them. Again, round up with the whole class and decide which are being used naturally.

4

> **Suggested answers**
> **Question 1:** can be answered directly
> **Question 2:** opener 2
> **Question 3:** openers 1 and 5
> **Question 4:** openers 1, 4 and 5
> **Question 5:** openers 1 and 5

Note: This is a good moment to do the Pronunciation section on sentence stress on page 74, which is based on Dominic's answers in Exercise 5.

5

> **Answers**
> 2, 5, 4, 3

Extension idea Ask students to work in pairs and to take turns asking and answering the questions in Exercise 4. Tell them to use the openers when they answer.

6 Ask students to change partners for this exercise.

Note: This is a good moment to do the Key grammar section on conditionals on page 76, which is based on Dominic's answers in Exercise 5.

7

> **Answers**
> 1 c   2 a, c

Extension idea Ask students to work in small groups and to take turns paraphrasing something. The other students have to guess what word is being paraphrased. To give them an example, you can say: *It's a sort of train which you find in cities and which runs through tunnels.* (*Answer*: underground)

8

> **Answers**
> **Student 1** B, c   **Student 2** A, g   **Student 3** C, a
> **Student 4** D, e

9 Tell students who are asking the questions (or who are listening) to give feedback to their partner on:

- how they start each answer.
- whether they try to paraphrase if they don't know a word.
- whether they use stress to emphasise or contrast points.

Pronunciation
Sentence stress 3

1 Point out to students that speakers always stress the words they particularly want the listener to hear, so stress will reflect the message, the attitude or the contrasts the speaker wants to make.

> **Suggested answers**
> 1 When I was <u>younger</u>, I <u>hated</u> going to <u>see</u> them- yeah - I though it was <u>so</u> <u>boring</u>.
> 2 My sister's very <u>hard-working</u>. <u>She</u> knows what she <u>wants</u>, whereas <u>I'm</u> still trying to make some <u>decisions</u> about that.
>
> Dominic uses stress in sentence 1 to show how strongly he felt; in sentence 2 he uses stress for contrast.

2 Ask students to work in pairs and read the sentences first to decide where the stress would sound more natural. You can point out that, like actors reading a script, they have to guess the speaker's intention in each sentence to get the stress correct. After they have listened to check their answers, ask them to take turns to read the sentences again to practise the stress patterns.

> **Answers**
> 1 *all* (emphasising)
> 2 *Before, now* (contrasting)
> 3 *gran, own, so pleased* (emphasising)
> 4 *architects* (emphasising)
>   *mum, dad* (contrasting)

3 4 When speakers take turns to answer these questions, tell their partners to decide if they're using stress to emphasise or contrast.

Writing   Task 1

1 *As a warmer* With books closed, write on the board:

- *money*
- *family*
- *friends*
- *health*
- *possessions*
- *free-time activities*
- *being successful*

Ask students to work in small groups and decide which three are most important for happiness. Are there any other things they would add to the list?

Tell students they are going to work on a task for Writing Task 1 based on a survey of happiness. Before that, they should do the exam round-up in the book.

> **Answers**
> 1 20   2 not always   3 should not   4 should
> 5 should not   6 your own words   7 need

2 To remind students of good exam technique, elicit what they should do when they first approach a writing task (i.e. underline the key ideas in the writing task). Ask them to do this. (*Suggested underlining*: What they think would make them happiest / extent / satisfied with lives)

- Elicit the meaning of 'extent'. (*Answer*: how much)
- Students should then do the exercise in the book. When they have finished, they should join with another pair and compare answers.

> **Answers**
> **1** They are linked in terms of topic. They have age groups in common.
> **2** How health and money contribute to people's happiness levels at different ages.
> **3** Life satisfaction for men and women at different ages.
> **4** Chart 1: Different things make people happy at different ages.
> Chart 2: Older and younger people are happiest, while middle-aged people are least happy.
> **5** It doesn't matter, but it might work best to start with the single trend, as this is more global.

3 Before students look at the exercise, elicit what an Exam 1 introductory paragraph should contain. (*Suggested answer*: a brief statement of what both graphs are about and what each graph in particular shows.) After students have done that, they should do the exam round-up in the book.

> **Answers**
> **1** a, b   **2** a   **3** a, c

Extension idea Ask students to work in pairs and analyse the three paragraphs. You can write the following questions on the board:

- *How is each paragraph different?*
- *Which do you think is best and why?*

(*Suggested answers*: Paragraph a is the best because it introduces the themes of both graphs. It then refers to factors and age groups when describing the first graph and levels and ages when describing the second graph. These are the key points in the two graphs, so the reader has a picture of how the graphs might look. Paragraph b starts well – although the words are copied. The second sentence does not mean anything and is unclear. The third sentence is true but the reader still has no idea what is on the graph. Paragraph c contains no introductory statement to help the reader. The description of both graphs is incomplete and slightly confusing.)

4

> **Answers**
> The student is summarising the second graph.
> The following parts should be circled: the start of each line at age 15–20; the point where both lines meet at age 41–50; the end of the lines at age 61–70.)

5 Elicit why the writer uses words like *it*, *this* and *their*. (*Answer*: to avoid repetition of things already mentioned)

> **Answers**
> **1** the trend in life satisfaction   **2** women's
> **3** between the ages of 15 and 20   **4** the scores'
> **5** the scores

6 Before students do this exercise, go through the Language reference on page 106 on reference devices. Point out that in English, it is good style to avoid repeating the same nouns and verbs too often, and using these devices helps with this.

> **Answers**
> **1** them (the youngest age group)   **2** this (55%)
> **3** it (this figure)   **4** their (the 15–24 age group's)
> **5** they (the 15–24 age group)   **6** these (money, health)   **7** one (one of the two trends)
> **8** their (people's)   **9** it (happiness)

Extension idea 1 Ask students to match the information in the paragraphs with the first chart. Ask them if all the important points have been covered.

Extension idea 2 Ask students to cover the charts in Exercise 2.

- Ask them to read the paragraphs carefully and draw a bar chart based only on the information contained in the paragraph.
- They then compare their charts with other students.
- Finally, they uncover the charts in Exercise 2 and compare theirs with the original to decide if the paragraph contains all the important information.

7

> **Answers**
>
> **1** They are linked in terms of topic. Both are about happiness levels among married people (but while the first graph compares this with happiness levels among unmarried people, the second looks at the effect of children on happiness levels).
>
> **2** Trends for four different age groups.
>
> **3** Trends for three different situations: with children under 18; with children over 18; with no children.
>
> **4 Chart 1**: levels are fairly flat, but the 50–64 age group is slightly less happy.
>
> **Chart 2**: levels are also quite flat, but couples with children over 18 are slightly less happy.
>
> **5** It is more logical to start with the first chart and then introduce children into the picture afterwards.

Extension idea Ask students to work in small groups and look at the instructions and the charts, and to suggest how they can use their own words instead of the words in the task. When they have finished, round up with the whole class to pool ideas. (See sample answer in Exercise 8.)

8 If you ask students to do the writing task for homework, ask them to do it under exam conditions (i.e. within a time limit of 20 minutes and trying to write at least 150 words). Remind them to set aside time at the end for reading and checking their answer for accuracy.

> **Sample answer**
>
> The charts show the percentage of people in the United States who are happy, divided into age groups, marital status and whether or not they have children.
>
> According to the charts, 44 to 45 percent of married people in ages ranging from 18 to 29, 30 to 39 and 65 plus are happy, while slightly fewer (40 percent) of those in the 50 to 64 age group are happy. In contrast, only 21 to 22 percent of unmarried people are happy in all age groups, apart from those aged 65 and over. Here, there is a significant difference, with 34 percent of people being happy.
>
> Having children appears to have little effect on happiness levels. The percentage of happy married people with children under 18 is 44 percent, while it is 43 percent for those without children and 41 percent for couples with children over 18.
>
> Overall, happiness levels in the US are below 50 percent. However married people tend to be happier than unmarried people, whether or not they have children.
>
> (166 words)

Key grammar
Zero, first and second conditionals

1 Tell students that conditionals will help boost their scores in the Speaking and Writing tests, because they will provide evidence that students can use complex sentence structures.

> **Answers**
> 1 c   2 b   3 a

2 Elicit from students that sentence 1 is second conditional, sentence 2 is first conditional and. that sentence 3 is zero conditional. Point out that the combination of tenses is important: if they use different tenses, the meaning changes. Go through the Language reference on page 106 with students and show how these example sentences match with the explanation there.

> **Answers**
> **1** *would* + verb in main clause + past simple in *if* clause
>
> **2** present simple in *if* clause + future simple in main clause
>
> **3** present simple in both clauses

3 Tell students to refer to the Language reference on page 106 while doing this exercise.

> **Answers**
> **2** would/might like   **3** was/were
> **4** don't plan   **5** won't/will not pass
> **6** stopped/could stop   **7** had   **8** will find out

4 Tell students that although IELTS candidates often make mistakes, they should not avoid using conditional sentences, as credit is given in the exam for trying to use complex sentences. However, students need to keep the rules for forming conditional sentences firmly in mind, especially the tenses.

> **Answers**
> **2** agreed   **3** will   **4** don't   **5** are
> **6** will never understand

Unit 7 photocopiable activity: Lie detection
Time: 30-40 minutes

Objectives
- To encourage oral fluency by answering questions
- To practise using 'openers'
- To revise vocabulary related to feelings and attitudes
- To revise zero, first and second conditionals

Before class

You will need one photocopy of the activity page on page 80 for each student.

In class

❶ *As a warmer* Ask students: *Do you think you would be able to tell if someone else was lying?*

- Explain that as a class, you are going to conduct a psychological experiment to investigate lie detection. Hand out an activity page on page 80 to each student and ask them to complete exercise 1. Check answers with the whole class.

> **Answers**
> 1 b 2 a 3 f 4 c 5 d 6 e

❷ Tell students to do exercise 2 alone. Point out that they do not need to use conditionals to complete this list of extra questions. Be ready to help with question forms if needed. With weaker classes, elicit some of the best questions and write them on the board.

❸

> **Answers**
> 1 speaking 2 see 3 sorry 4 mean 5 interesting

❹ Explain that before starting the experiment, students should first be aware of all the different ways in which lying could be detected. Ask students to work in pairs to brainstorm ideas and write them in the box. Conduct feedback with the whole class.

> **Possible answers**
> body language clues, e.g. looking away from the interviewer, moving hands nervously, coughing
>
> verbal clues, e.g. hesitating, being vague about details, avoiding giving detailed personal examples

❺ Re-arrange the pairs so that each student is now working with a new partner who they will interview for the experiment. Ask students to decide silently if they are going to tell the truth or lie throughout the interview. If they choose to lie, they must give false answers to every question, not just some. Give them a few minutes to prepare their thoughts.

- Students take turns in their new pairs to interview one another, using the questions and openers they prepared earlier. Each interview should last about five minutes. Emphasise that, during the interviews, no comments should be made about whether lies are being told. During the interview, monitor the students' use of conditionals and/ or sentence stress, so that you can give feedback later on.

- Once all the interviews have finished, ask students to tell their partners whether they suspect them of lying during the interview. They must give reasons for their theories, and match their observations against their list of ideas brainstormed in exercise 4.

- Finally, students reveal to their partners whether they were lying or not. If there is time, discuss what conclusions can be drawn from the class experiment.

Unit 7 photocopiable activity
Lie detection

❶ Match the sentence halves to make six questions. Use your knowledge of conditionals to help you.

1	If you are feeling anxious or upset,	a	what would it be?
2	If you could change one thing about yourself,	b	how do you calm yourself down?
3	If a friend's behaviour was irritating you,	c	what helps you to make up your mind?
4	If you have to make a difficult decision,	d	how would you solve it?
5	If you had a problem in a relationship,	e	how do you help them?
6	If you are concerned about a family member,	f	how would you let them know?

❷ You are going to interview a partner. Prepare five more questions to ask about relationships.

1 ....

2 ....

3 ....

4 ....

5 ....

❸ To help you deal with an interviewer's questions, you can use 'openers' to start your answer. Complete the following 'openers' with words from the box.

see   interesting   sorry   speaking   mean

1 Generally .... , I …

2 Let me .... , it's hard to remember …

3 I'm .... , can you repeat the question?

4 It depends on what you .... by …

5 That's an .... question …

❹ Work with a partner. Brainstorm all the possible signs that a person could be lying. Make notes in the box below.

```




```

❺ You are now going to conduct an experiment in lie detection. Your teacher will give you instructions.

Complete IELTS Bands 5–6.5 by Guy Brook-Hart and Vanessa Jakeman with David Jay © Cambridge University Press 2012 PHOTOCOPIABLE

Vocabulary extension

Unit 7

Abbreviations: n/pln = noun / plural noun; v = verb; adj = adjective; adv = adverb; p = phrase;
T/I = transitive/intransitive; C/U = countable/uncountable

adolescence *n* [U] the period of time in someone's life between being a child and an adult

attitude *n* [C] how you think or feel about something and how this makes you behave

be supportive *vp* to give help and encouragement to someone

bring up a child *vp* to care for a child until it is an adult

characteristics *pln* [C] the qualities or features of someone or something

childhood memories *pln* [C] the things that you remember from when you were a child

close friend *n* [C] Your close friends are the people you know very well and like a lot.

counselling *n* [U] the job or process of listening to someone and giving them advice about their problems

divorce *n* [C] when two people officially stop being married

expression *n* [C] the look on someone's face showing what they feel or think

extended family *n* [C] a family unit which includes grandmothers, grandfathers, aunts and uncles, etc. in addition to parents, children, bothers and sisters

fall out *p* to argue with someone and stop being friendly with them

family celebration *n* [C] a special social event such as a party, for family members

family life *n* [U] the life that someone has with their family

family reunion *n* [C] a social event where family members who have not seen each other for some time come together

get married *p* to begin a legal relationship with someone as their husband or wife

gender differences *n* [C] the things that are different about males and females

have a (shy) personality *vp* to be a (shy) type of person

household chores/tasks *pln* [C] jobs that have to be done as part of running a home

have a good/bad relationship with someone *vp* If two people have a good/bad relationship, they like/dislike each other and behave well/badly towards each other.

in the community *np* Things that happen or exist in the community, happen or exist among the group of people that live in a particular area.

look up to someone *vp* to admire and respect someone

lucky charm *n* [C] an object that is thought to bring good luck

mentor *n* [C] an experienced person who gives help and advice to someone with less experience

nuclear family *n* [C] a family consisting of two parents and their children, but not including aunts, uncles, grandparents, etc.

optimist *n* [C] someone who always believes that good things will happen

outgoing *adj* someone who is outgoing is friendly, talks a lot, and enjoys meeting people

pessimist *n* [C] Someone who always believes that bad things will happen.

sensitive *adj* able to understand what people are feeling and deal with them in a way that does not upset them

show off *p* to try to make people admire your abilities or achievements in a way which other people find annoying

sibling rivalry *n* [C] competition and arguments between brothers and sisters

single-parent family *n* [C] a family where only one parent lives at home and looks after the children

well-being *n* [U] the state of being healthy, happy, and comfortable

Unit 8 Fashion and design

Unit objectives

- **Reading Section 3:** practising scanning; multiple choice; Yes / No / Not Given; introducing the matching sentence-endings task
- **Listening Section 4:** listening for synonyms or paraphrases; practising sentence completion
- **Speaking Parts 2 and 3:** making comparisons; providing a list of points; supporting a view with reasons; structuring a Part 3 answer
- **Pronunciation:** linking and pausing
- **Vocabulary:** *dress* (uncountable) / *dress(es)* (countable) / *clothes* / *cloth*
- **Writing Part 2:** discussing two opinions, including own opinion; introducing other people's opinions; writing the concluding paragraph
- **Key grammar:** tenses and verb forms with time conjunctions

Starting off

❶ *As a warmer* Write these on the board:

- *to go shopping*
- *to come to class*
- *to do a sporting activity*
- *to go to a wedding*

Ask students to work in small groups. Ask:

- *What clothes do you wear on these occasions. Why?*
- *Do you think your clothes reflect your personality? If so, how?*

❷ Students may only know the name of traditional dress in their own language, in which case they should paraphrase to describe it.

Reading   Section 3

❶ *Background* The portrait, painted by John Singer Sargent in 1889, is of the famous 19th-century British actress Ellen Terry in her role as Lady Macbeth, wearing her 'Beetlewing' dress. The portrait is in the Tate Gallery in London. During this period, the use of beetle wings to make dresses and handbags was popular in wealthy circles. The wings were often imported from India.

❷ Ask students to glance at the article and the tasks which follow before they read. Give them strictly three minutes to scan for three reasons why the dress is being restored.

Answers

It is about a project to restore a famous actress's dress.

It is unique; a famous actress wore it; it is in a painting; the wearer is known; it has historical value.

❸ *Alternative treatment* With multiple-choice questions it is important to train students to read the question, then to read and understand the relevant section of the passage before reading the options (A–D). Reading the options before reading the passage often confuses students, with the result that they choose the wrong answer. To train them appropriately, follow the treatment below.

For **Questions 1–6**, write the following questions on the board and ask students to copy them into their notebooks (they shouldn't look at Exercise 3 in their books at this point).

1 *What do you learn about Ellen Terry in the first paragraph?*

2 *What is the writer's purpose in paragraph 2?*

3 *What was the main effect of the Lyceum productions?*

4 *In the fourth paragraph, what comparison does the writer make between Sargent's portrait and the Beetlewing dress?*

5 *Why, according to Zenzie, is the Beetlewing project particularly special?*

6 *What would be the most suitable title for the article?*

Then tell students to:

- underline key ideas in each question. (*Suggested underlining:* 1 *learn about Ellen Terry* 2 *writer's purpose* 3 *main effect of the Lyceum productions* 4 *comparison ... Sargent's portrait and the Beetlewing dress* 5 *project ... particularly special* 6 *most suitable title*)

- read the passage and underline the words which give the answer to each of the questions.

- work in pairs and explain their answers using their own words.

- choose the correct option for each question on page 79 in the Student's Book without reading the passage again.

Talk through this procedure with students, explaining why they have done it, so that they can do it themselves in the exam.

For **Questions 7–10**, elicit from students how they should approach these. (*Answers*: underlining key ideas, underlining words which echo words in the passage and therefore make the relevant section of the passage quick to find, etc.) If necessary, refer them to the Exam advice.

Answers

1 C (*She knew the power of presentation and carefully cultivated her image.*)

2 B (*The effect had been achieved using hundreds of wings from beetles – insects that have hard shiny bodies and wings that change colour in the light.*)

3 A (*Some people were critical, but they missed the point. The innovations sold tickets and brought new audiences to see masterpieces that they would never otherwise have seen.*)

4 D (*But while the painting remains almost as fresh as the day it was painted, the years have not been so kind to the dress.*)

5 B (*But it's quite unusual to know who actually wore a garment. That's the thing that makes the Beetlewing project so special.*)

6 B (*The subheading and main ideas in text.*)

7 NOT GIVEN (*The National Trust is mentioned, but nothing is said about whether or not it conducted any research prior to the project.*)

8 YES (*Then Zenzie and the National Trust will decide how far back to take the reconstruction, as some members feel that even the most recent changes are now part of the history of the dress.*)

9 NOT GIVEN (*The writer states the timing but gives no view on it.*)

10 NO (*Unlike many other actresses, she valued her costumes because she kept and reused them time and time again.*)

❹ Matching sentence endings tests students' ability to scan the passage for words relating to each sentence beginning and then to understand in detail what is said, before matching the idea or information with a paraphrased ending.

Suggested underlining

11 Pictures   **12** special machine   **13** net material
14 visible on one side

A show how the team did the repairs   **B** reduce the time   **C** clean the top layer   **D** demonstrate the quality   **E** match/original fabric   **F** show where the dress needs repair work

❺ Before doing these questions:

- elicit what subject all the sentences are about (the repair of the dress).
- tell students to scan for that section of the passage.

When students have finished, ask them to:

- read their answers again to make sure they are grammatical and fit what they have understood from their reading.
- compare answers in pairs.

Point out the relevant words in the passage which gave them the answers.

Answers

11 F (*Zenzie … will conduct a thorough investigation to help determine what changes have been made to the dress and when. This will involve close examination of the dress for signs of damage and wear, and will be aided by comparing it with John Singer Sargent's painting and contemporary photographs.*)

12 C (*The first stages in the actual restoration will involve delicate surface cleaning, using a small vacuum suction device.*)

13 E (*'It's going to be extraordinarily difficult because the original cloth is quite stretchy, so we've deliberately chosen net because that has a certain amount of flexibility in it too,' says Zenzie.*)

14 A (*… we'll retain all the evidence on the reverse so that future experts will be able to see exactly what we've done.*)

Vocabulary

dress (uncountable) / *dress(es)* (countable) / *clothes* / *cloth*

❶ Check that students have noted the grammatical difference between the two words *dress* – countable and uncountable. Elicit the difference in meaning between *a formal dress* and *formal dress*. Tell students to pay extra attention when using these words.

Answers
1 clothes   2 dress

Extension idea Ask students to write four of their own sentences using *dress* [U], *dress* [C], *clothes* and *cloth*.

Answers
2 ~~cloth~~/clothes/clothing   3 ~~dresses~~/dress/clothing
4 ~~dresses~~/dress/clothing   5 ✓

3 These questions are in the style of Speaking Part 1.

Alternative treatment Ask one student to take the role of 'examiner' and the other to be the candidate. When they have finished, ask them to change roles and do the exercise again.

Listening   Section 4

1 *As a warmer* With books closed, ask students to imagine they are teachers telling IELTS candidates about the Listening Paper. They work in small groups. What information can they give?

When they open their books, ask:

- *Is there any information which you missed?*
- *Is there other important information not mentioned in the round up?*

> **Answers**
> **2** questions   **3** break   **4** ten   **5** one
> **6** answers   **7** ✓   **8** ten

2

> **Suggested answers**
> **1 A** an ancient Japanese coat
> **B** a modern bag
> **C** a modern quilt
> **3 A** museum
> **B** shop/home
> **C** shop/home

Extension idea Ask students for a personal reaction:

- *Do you admire any of these things?*
- *Would you like to own one yourself?*

3 Tell students that listening for synonyms or paraphrases helps in the same way as listening for signals did in Unit 7: if they recognise the synonym, they will know that the answer is coming.

> **Answers**
> **2** in the beginning   **3** fabrics   **4** join
> **5** designs   **6** wore   **7** know how to do
> **8** not needed   **9** modern   **10** old clothes

Extension idea Ask students to work in pairs and think of their own synonyms or paraphrases for the following words from each question (you can write them on the board): 1 *word* 2 *decorative* 3 *parts* 4 *produced* 5 *called* 6 *wore* 7 *essential* 8 *began* 9 *patterns* 10 *not as.* You can round up and get suggestions from the whole class. (*Suggested answers*: 1 term 2 beautiful/ornamental 3 regions 4 made 5 with the name of/named 6 dressed in 7 important 8 started 9 designs 10 less)

4 Before listening:

- tell students they will hear this once only as in the exam.
- ask them to quickly decide what type of information they need for each gap.
- tell them to look at the gaps carefully. In some they will need a plural noun; can they identify which?

After listening:

- tell students to read their answers through to check they make sense.
- tell them that in the exam, they will have time to transfer their answers to a separate answer sheet. Give 2½ minutes to transfer their answers to a separate page in the notebooks. Tell them that this is important to practise, because many candidates make spelling mistakes when transferring their answers. Ask students to compare their answers in pairs. Then play the recording again to check.

Round up with the whole class to check spelling. If students offer more than one way of spelling an answer, write the alternatives on the board and ask them to identify which is correct.

> **Answers**
> **1** little stitches   **2** functional   **3** wool
> **4** (many) layers   **5** sea wave   **6** firemen / fire men
> **7** farmer   **8** rail travel   **9** diamond   **10** collectors

5 *Extension idea* You can personalise this by asking:

- *Does your family keep old family things from the past? What things and why?*

Speaking   Parts 2 and 3

1 *As a warmer* Ask students to work in pairs and imagine they are going to give advice to someone who doesn't know anything about the IELTS exam. What advice would they give about how to do Speaking Part 2?

> **Answers**
> **2** F (There is only one topic; if you have no experience of it, make something up.)
> **3** F (The points guide you, but you can cover them in any order.)
> **4** F (The examiner will know if you have memorised a talk and you will lose marks.)
> **5** T
> **6** T
> **7** F (Part 1 topics are personal and straightforward; Part 3 topics are general and abstract.)
> **8** F (Both parts last four to five minutes.)
> **9** T
> **10** T

❷ *Alternative treatment* Since this is the last unit before students do the exam, they can do the task under exam conditions:

- Say to students: *Now I'm going to give you a topic and I'd like you to talk about it for one to two minutes. Before you talk, you'll have one minute to think about what you're going to say. You can make some notes if you wish.*
- Ask students to look at the prompts in the book. Give one minute to make notes and prepare what they will say.
- While they are preparing, write on the board:

  Do you think you'll visit it again? Would you recommend it to your friends?
- At the end of the minute, ask students to work in pairs and give their talks. Give two minutes for this.
- When they finish speaking, their partner should ask the questions on the board.
- They then change roles and repeat the task.

❸ Tell students that different Part 3 questions may need different strategies in order to answer them well. So when the examiner asks a question, students should think to themselves: *What type of strategy should I use to answer?*

> **Answers**
> **a** 3   **b** 1   **c** 1, 2, 3

Explain that in answering each question, students could do more. For example, for question 3, they could also support a view and give reasons. However, this exercise aims to show that students need to think carefully about the type of answer the examiner expects. If students are asked about benefits and they do not give any, then they will not have answered the question.

Ask students to brainstorm ideas for questions 1–3.

❹ 🎧 Deal with each question one by one. After playing each answer twice for students to answer the questions in the book, elicit:

- what points each candidate makes.
- relevant vocabulary from Lin's answers particularly, and write examples on the board. Students will be able to use them later. (*Suggested vocabulary*: *experience, environment, exhibits, activities, displays, entertain, ancient objects, interactive*)
- how Lin structures her answers in each case.

> **Answers**
>
> | | Who ... | David | Lin |
> |---|---|:---:|:---:|
> | **question 1** | **a** presents benefits? | ✔ | ✔ |
> | | **b** explains benefits? | ✗ | ✔ |
> | | **c** keeps strictly to the question? | ✗ | ✔ |
> | | **d** structures their answer clearly? | ✗ | ✔ |
> | **question 2** | **a** presents a view? | ✔ | ✔ |
> | | **b** gives reasons? | ✗ | ✔ |
> | | **c** uses general, not personal, arguments? | ✗ | ✔ |
> | | **d** structures their answer clearly? | ✗ | ✔ |
> | **question 3** | **a** makes comparisons? | ✗ | ✔ |
> | | **b** supports points? | ✔ | ✔ |
> | | **c** covers past and present? | ✗ | ✔ |
> | | **d** structures their answer clearly? | ✔ | ✔ |

❺

> **Suggested answers**
>
> Overall, Lin produces the best answers. Her responses are structured well, using appropriate discourse markers to signal her key points. She links her supporting ideas to these, using a range of connectives. She clearly introduces benefits and explains these, and makes comparison.
>
> David produces some benefits in a list. Some of his points are very general, and the sentence about expense is not relevant. David's answer contains a brief explanation, but his point is repetitive and undeveloped. He also begins to talk about himself, rather than about people in general. David uses less vocabulary and it is quite simple: *fun, prefer, football, happy,* etc. His structures are also simpler than Lin's.

Note: This is a good moment to do the Pronunciation section on linking and pausing on page 83, which is based on Lin's answers in Exercise 4.

❻ Give students a little more time to think and prepare on their own. Point out that they needn't copy Lin's answers, but should express their own ideas.

Extension idea Once students have finished and given each other feedback, ask them to change partners and take turns to ask and answer the questions again using the checklist for feedback.

7 Students can treat this exercise as exam practice. In this case, they should work in pairs and one student should work with their book closed while the other student asks them the questions. When they have finished, they should change roles.

Alternative treatment Ask students to prepare their answers in pairs. They can:

- check back to see if there are any words or phrases they have seen in the unit which they could use.
- discuss how they can answer each question.
- take turns to ask and answer the questions and give feedback.

Pronunciation
Linking and pausing

1 Tell students that their English will sound more natural if they can link words correctly. Play the question several times. Ask students individually to repeat what the examiner says to see how linking works.

> **Answer**
> b

2 When students listen to check their answers, they should listen several times.

> **Answer**
> **1** First of all // they can experience things directly // you know // they're not in the classroom any more // they're in a different environment.
> **3** I don't think there's any doubt // that museums are much better at educating children now … In the past I think museums had a different function // um // they were just places to keep ancient objects // like coins or pots // but now they're // well there are many interactive displays.

3

Extension idea Ask students to choose one question from Speaking Exercise 3 and write their answer to it. Ask them then to mark where they would put links and pauses. They then work in small groups and read their answers to their partners. Their partners can say who is speaking most naturally (and why).

Writing   Task 2

1 *As a warmer* Ask students to work alone and write down the three main difficulties they have when they do Writing Task 2 (e.g. *I don't have enough time*).

Then ask them to work in small groups. Ask them to take turns to present their difficulties and the reasons for them.

Their partners should make suggestions for them to deal with their difficulties.

When they have done the exam round-up, you will perhaps need to explain that:

- many students spend too long doing Task 1, with the result that they don't have time to do well on Task 2.
- they can gain twice as many marks on Task 2 as Task 1, so it is important that they leave 40 minutes for this task. (Avoid recommending that they do Task 2 first. This can have a more negative effect on their score if they end up with no time for Task 1 at all.)
- they will lose marks if they do not reach the minimum word count, but they should not aim to increase their word count by copying from the task rubric, as these words will not be counted.
- they can use words from the graphics and headings and use isolated words and phrases from the rubric, but they should bear in mind that they get credit for using their own words where they can.
- they need to express their opinion clearly in Task 2 and maintain their position throughout the answer.
- the examiner will mark the answer objectively: the examiner will assess whether the opinions are supported logically with reasons and examples, but not relate the student's opinions to his/her own.
- the examiner will look at the overall structure and coherence of the answer, including whether it is divided logically into paragraphs and whether main ideas are clearly highlighted and supported within paragraphs.
- candidates will limit their possibilities of achieving a high Band score for grammar if they 'play safe' and use simple structures and vocabulary.

> **Answers**
> **1** 40   **2** twice as many marks as
> **3** you will lose marks   **4** must   **5** needn't   **6** is
> **7** try to use complex language and risk making mistakes

2 Before students read the task, elicit that they should underline the key ideas.

> **Suggested underlining**
> Some people argue that fashion items cost too much money.
> Others say that this is acceptable because fashion is an important part of life.

3 *Extension idea 1* After they have discussed how the different people might feel about the opinions, ask students to work in small groups with different partners and discuss:

- how they personally feel about the two opinions and why.
- which people on the list they think they would agree with and why.

Round up with the whole class, perhaps turning the topic into a class discussion and finishing off with a vote to find out which opinion is the most popular.

Extension idea 2 As a follow-up to questions 4 and 5 in the exam round-up, ask students if it is acceptable to answer giving a third opinion, not just agreeing with one or other of the opinions in the question. (*Answer*: Yes, this is in the task instructions – *Discuss both these views and give your own opinion.*)

> **Answers**
> Some people say that prices should be lower in shops …
> However, there are other people who say they are happy to pay for designer clothes.
> The writer's opinion is in the second and fourth paragraphs.

Extension idea Ask students:

- *Do the opinions repeat the same words as in the question, or do they express the same idea using different words?* (*Answer*: they express the same idea using different words.)
- *Which is better?* (*Answer*: to use your own words.)
- *Is the writer's position clear in the answer? Why is this important?* (*Answer*: if you don't express your own opinion clearly and stick to your argument throughout the answer, you're not answering the question and you will lose marks for content.)

> **Answers**
> **Suggesting what might be someone else's view**
> X might argue that
> (in sample answer) (Celebrities) … might say that
>
> **giving a clear opinion of your own**
> Personally I agree
> (in sample answer) Personally, I think; I can understand their point of view
>
> **introducing an opposing argument**
> Other people disagree
> (in sample answer) However, there are other people who say; On the other hand
>
> **giving someone else's view**
> In X's opinion; According to X
> (in sample answer) Some people say that; …
> (fashion designers) would also argue that;
> According to people in the fashion business

Extension idea Ask students to choose one phrase from each column and write their own sentences on the topic using the phrases. They then compare their sentences in small groups.

7 You can ask students to look at concluding paragraphs from sample answers in Units 2, 4 and 6 in the Student's Book to see which items are appropriate.

> **Answers**
> **1, 2** (if brief and in different words); **4, 5** (only if relevant); and **7** (no new points should be included)

8 ***Alternative treatment*** Ask students to write their own concluding paragraph based on what they chose in Exercise 7. (They will need to close their books or cover this part of the page to do this.) They then compare their answers with the paragraph shown in Exercise 8.

> **Answers**
> 7, 1, 4

9 Make sure that students have underlined the key ideas in the task before they start (they should now be doing this automatically).

- Tell students they needn't include all the people or organisations in their answer. They should perhaps choose three or four. (*Suggested answers*: employers; professional workers; unskilled workers; the general public; customers; job applicants)
- Ask students to form their own opinions before they plan.

Alternative treatment Turn this into a class discussion. To help students focus on the issues, you can ask:

- *Why do organisations want employees to dress smartly? What does it say about the organisation?*
- *What sort of organisations expect their employees to dress smartly?*
- *What sort of organisations worry less about appearance?*
- *Is there any relationship between quality of work and appearance?*
- *How do you think employees feel about dressing smartly? Do they prefer to, or would they prefer not to?*
- *What do customers think?*

Note: This is a good moment to do the Grammar section on time conjunctions on page 85.

10 Sometimes on an exam-preparation course, it is beneficial to ask students to do one of their writing tasks in class:

Fashion and design (87)

- it replicates an exam situation – students can concentrate and work without distraction.
- it allows you to observe and pick up on bad habits (e.g. students who don't plan, students who don't read through what they've written, students who try to make a fair copy which they won't have time for in the exam).

Tell students when they write, they should:

- leave enough space to make corrections where necessary.
- cross out mistakes and write their correction above.

> **Sample answer**
>
> Traditionally, people who work in offices have worn smart clothes to work. No one thought about changing this until a few companies brought out a 'casual clothes' policy. Now suits have become less common in some organisations; but is it wise to allow employees to wear casual clothes?
>
> Insurance companies that have a strong public image would argue that they need to have smart employees in order to promote their products. Before they meet a client, sales people often check their appearance because they know that customers will not buy things from them if they are badly dressed. Some banks and airlines are so concerned about image that they provide uniforms for their staff. Personally, I think this is a good idea. When someone is doing business, jeans and T-shirts just seem too casual.
>
> On the other hand, if you work in an IT company and you never go out, do you need to dress well? A technician might argue that the important thing is how well they do their job, not what they wear. But after a visitor has seen a shabby employee in the office, they might decide to take their business to another firm.
>
> When I was a student, I thought that clothes did not matter. Now that I have left college and started working in a company, I think that I should take pride in my work. If I am dressed well, I feel more efficient, and that may even improve my work.
>
> I would conclude that being smart is important. Some employees may say they feel unhappy about this, but they can easily change and wear something more informal when they have left work. The office is a different environment.
>
> (285 words)

Key grammar
Time conjunctions, *until / when / before / after*

1 Remind students that they will gain marks by writing complex sentences appropriately. This section helps them to do this.

> **Answers**
> **2** Before / Until **3** After / When **4** when
> **5** until / before

2 Ask students to do questions 2 and 3 in pairs.

- Then elicit answers from the whole class and write their different suggestions on the board. Ask the class to decide which is correct.
- Ask students to do questions 4–7 alone, then check again with their partners.

> **Answers**
> **2** Staff cannot smoke until they have left / leave the building.
>
> **3** After you have worn casual clothes to work, it is hard to wear a suit.
>
> **4** Some people don't go shopping until the sales start / have started.
>
> **5** Employees all look the same when they put on a uniform.
>
> **6** Before designer brands were introduced, customers spent less money on clothes.
>
> **7** When I have spent all my money, I (will) go home.

3

> **Answers**
> **2** bought **3** we graduate **4** we achieve
> **5** grow up **6** reach

Extension idea Ask students to look at Exercise 10 in Writing Part 2 and write three sentences they could use with time conjunctions when answering the task.

Vocabulary and grammar review Unit 7

Answers

Vocabulary

1 **2** reassuring **3** irritating **4** persuasive **5** bored **6** concerned

2 **2** the age **3** age group **4** the ages **5** aged **6** age **7** the age **8** age group

Grammar

❸ 2 would say   3 doesn't   4 met   5 think   6 cannot
7 is   8 might   9 you find

❹ In every society, people need to build relationships with ~~another~~ **other** people. These relationships can take place at work, school or home. Wherever ~~it~~ **they** occur, it is important that people understand each other. An organisation will not function well if ~~their~~ **its** members are unhappy. Good managers understand ~~the~~ **this** point and make sure they reward employees for good work. In fact, when you take time to understand what people want and why they want ~~them~~ **it**, it is usually possible to solve most problems. ~~These~~ **This** results in a happy environment where people progress well.

Vocabulary and grammar review Unit 8

Answers

Vocabulary

❶ 2 a   3 b   4 h   5 g   6 c   7 f   8 d

❷ 2 material   3 Celebrities   4 suit   5 uniform
6 dressed   7 sari   8 fashionable

❸ 2 dress   3 cloth   4 dress   5 cloth   6 clothes
7 dresses   8 clothes

Grammar

❹ 2 have bought   3 became   4 have been   5 wash
6 buy   7 had   8 have been   9 we'll

Time conjunctions: *when, until, before, after*

Unit 8 photocopiable activity: Visual values

Time: 30-40 minutes

Objectives

- To practise supporting a view with reasons
- To practise the use of time conjunctions
- To recycle vocabulary related to design and the arts
- To practise dealing with data in a graph format

Before class

You will need one photocopy of the activity page on page 90 for each student.

In class

❶ Ask students to read through the statements for each section in the survey and circle the correct option in italics. They do this alone and then check with a partner. Then go through the answers with the class.

> **Answers**
> 1 clothes   2 fashionably   3 I go   4 dress   5 visit
> 6 When   7 come   8 have looked   9 In   10 When
> 11 do   12 agree   13 When   14 am going   15 live
> 16 may

❷ Divide the class into two equal groups. Explain to students that they are going to conduct a survey to find out how interested they are in art and design.

❸ Ask each group to discuss follow-up questions they could ask to extend discussion during the survey. For example, for section 1: *How often do you go clothes shopping? How long do you spend in each shop?*

❹ Each student finds a partner from the other group and they work through the survey together, discussing each statement before agreeing which number best suits their partner. Encourage students not simply to write down numbers, but have an extended discussion using the questions they've prepared.

❺ As the students do the task, monitor their use of vocabulary related to design and the arts. You may also wish to focus on their use of linking and pausing.

❻ After at least 10 minutes, ask students to fill in the average score for their partner for each section, by adding up the four scores and dividing by four (rounding to the nearest whole number). They return to the original groups and share their results by calculating a group average for each section by adding up the average scores for each individual in the group and dividing by the number of group members. When they have worked out the group average for each section, they can plot this on the bar chart at the bottom of the sheet.

❼ Explain to students that they are now going to return to the person they interviewed and compare the results from the two groups. Before they do this, elicit phrases for introducing opinions and write them up the board (e.g. *According to X it's important to dress fashionably*). Encourage students to use these when they report their findings to their partner.

❽ Ask the class what conclusions they can draw about each group as a whole, before conducting a feedback session based on any errors you monitored during the interviews.

Extension idea As a follow-up writing task, students write a Task 1-style report comparing the findings for each group.

Visual values

Score (5=strongly agree,
1=strongly disagree)

Section 1: Fashion and clothing

I enjoy spending time buying ¹*clothes/cloth* and choosing what to wear.

I think it is important to dress ²*fashionably/fashionable* at work or at school.

Before ³*I'm going/I go* to a party or celebration, I spend a lot of time on my appearance.

I think that people who ⁴*dress/wear* well are more likely to be successful in life.

Average score for Section 1

Section 2: Interior Design

When I ⁵*will visit/visit* a friend's house, I look carefully at the furniture and decoration.

⁶*When/Until* you have an attractive home, your quality of life improves.

Before friends or neighbours ⁷*come/are coming* to my home, I take care to make sure that it looks good.

After you ⁸*have looked/will have looked* at someone's home, you can tell a lot about their life.

Average score for Section 2

Section 3: Art in society

⁹*According to/In* my opinion it is right for governments to spend money on artistic projects.

¹⁰*After/When* I have some free time, I visit museums and art galleries.

When people ¹¹*do/are doing* activities such as painting or dance, their health may improve.

Personally, I ¹²*agree/argue* that works of art in museums are an important part of national identity.

Average score for Section 3

Section 4: Architecture

¹³*When/Until* I visit a new city, I pay attention to the design and style of the buildings.

I often look up at the buildings around me when I ¹⁴*am going/go* to school or work.

When people ¹⁵*would live/live* and work in beautiful buildings, their lives are improved.

Some people ¹⁶*may/should* argue that architecture is unimportant, but I think it has a significant role to play in society.

Average score for Section 4

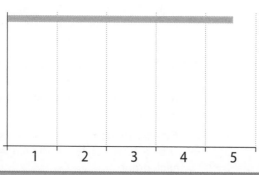

Bar chart illustrating the average level of interest of a group of IELTS students in various aspects of art and design.

Vocabulary extension

Unit 8

Abbreviations: n/pln = noun / plural noun; v = verb; adj = adjective; adv = adverb; p = phrase;
T/I = transitive/intransitive; C/U = countable/uncountable

accessories *pln* [C] small items that you wear with your main clothes, for example jewellery, bags, scarves or gloves

a good/bad fit *p* If a piece of clothing is a good/bad fit, it is the right/wrong shape and size for you.

bargain *n* [C] something that is sold for less than its usual price or its real value

celebrity culture *n* [U] a society in which famous people are admired very much

cotton *n* [U] cloth or thread that is produced from the cotton plant

crease-resistant *adj* Crease-resistant cloth does not leave lines when it is folded or crushed.

fashion icon *n* [C] a person who is admired by many people because they are extremely fashionable and stylish

hairstyle *n* [C] the style in which someone arranges their hair

jeans *n* [U] trousers made from denim (= a strong, usually blue, material)

look good in something *vp* If you look good in an item of clothing, it makes you look attractive.

on display *p* If something is on display, it is there for people to look at.

outdated / old-fashioned *adj* no longer fashionable

outfit *n* [C] a set of clothes for a particular event or activity

leather *n* [U] the skin of animals that is used to make things such as shoes and bags

machine-made *adj* made using a machine, rather than by hand

made to measure *adj* made specially to fit a particular person, room, etc.

size *n* [C] one of the different measurements in which things such as clothes are made

silk *n* [U] a light, smooth cloth made from fibres produced by a type of worm

put on *v T* If you put on clothes, you start to wear them.

set a trend *p* to cause something to become popular

take off *p* If you take off clothes, you remove them from your body.

tailor *n* [C] someone whose job is to make or repair clothes, especially men's clothes

to be made of *vp* If an object is made of something, it is formed from that substance.

try on *vp* If you try on clothes, you put them on to see if they fit and if they look good on you.

the sales *pln* a period of time when goods are sold at a lower price than usual

the retail industry *n* [U] all the companies involved in selling goods directly to customers

to suit someone (it suits / doesn't suit me) *p* If a piece of clothing, jewellery, makeup, etc. suits you, it makes you look good.

wardrobe *n* [C] 1. a large cupboard for keeping clothes in 2. [U] Someone's wardrobe is all the clothes that they own.

worn out *adj* Something that is worn-out is so old or has been used so much that it is damaged too much to repair.

❶ Match each word in the first column with a word/words in the second column to form a phrase.

0 give ....*d*....	**a** upset
1 make	**b** your feelings
2 tell	**c** a trend
3 express	**d** a definition
4 do	**e** a project
5 feel	**f** the truth
6 set	**g** friends

❷ Complete the description of the graph by writing one word or phrase from the box in each gap.

Age distribution of billionaires

aged	of age	age group	age of	ages

The graph shows how many billionaires there are in one country and which (**0**) ...*age group*... they belong to. Clearly, the largest group of billionaires, at 110, are (**1**) .... 60 to 69, while the smallest group is the 30–39 (**2**) .... Between these (**3**) .... the graph rises steadily. However, after the (**4**) .... 69, the number of billionaires declines – slightly at first and then quite sharply when people are over 79 years (**5**) .... There is only one billionaire under 30 and only three in the very oldest (**6**) ....

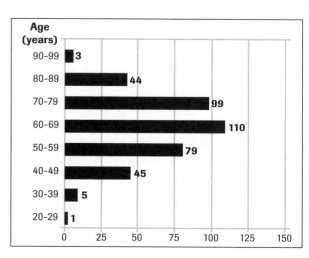

❸ Match each word in the first column with a word in the second column that has a similar meaning.

0 modern (adj) ....*c*....	**a** well-known
1 costumes (n)	**b** fabric
2 task (n)	**c** contemporary
3 mend (v)	**d** repair
4 material (n)	**e** garments
5 appearance (n)	**f** image
6 famous (adj)	**g** job

❹ Complete the sentences using words from the box.

~~image~~	mend	task	costumes	contemporary	exhibit	well-known

0 Fashion-conscious people are very concerned about their ......*image*...... .

1 Unfortunately, many ancient theatrical .... have been destroyed.

2 A lot of .... people have their clothes made by fashion designers.

3 Museums today .... some fascinating clothes from around the world.

4 These days, sports clothes are made using a wide range of .... materials.

5 In the past, people used to .... clothes, rather than buy new ones.

6 Making your own clothes is quite a difficult ....

❺ **Complete the sentences by writing one word from the box in each gap. There is one extra word that you do not need to use.**

~~her~~	it	you	them	others	they	ones	most

0 Unfortunately, Lucy didn't return the book I lent ....*her*......... last week.

1 There are about 10 million millionaires in the world and most of .... live in the US.

2 The photographs I took of my college are better than the .... in the brochure.

3 When I took my driving test, I didn't expect to pass ....

4 Some people spend a lot of money, while .... prefer to save.

5 Being an optimist doesn't mean that .... are always happy!

6 Special occasions are important because .... help people stay in touch with one another.

❻ **Choose the best alternative (A, B or C) for each of these sentences.**

0 If you buy a small apartment, you ....*B*......... fewer possessions.
   A needed   **B** will need   **C** would need

1 Unless museums offer interactive experiences, children .... an interest in them.
   A developed   **B** will not develop   **C** would not develop

2 Mike hasn't got in touch yet – unless .... his call.
   A I'm missing   **B** I've missed   **C** I could miss

3 If advertisements were less persuasive, people .... more money in their bank accounts.
   A might have   **B** have   **C** had

4 People don't usually talk to you about their personal life unless they .... you well.
   A know   **B** knew   **C** might know

5 If I had more artistic talent, I .... my own clothes.
   A designed   **B** will design   **C** would design

❼ **Correct the underlined mistake in each sentence.**

0 My father is doing a Fine Art course when he <u>will retire</u>. ......*retires*......

1 I always think about what I'm going to wear before I <u>went</u> out. ....

2 Until I worked in an office, I <u>wear</u> very unfashionable clothes. ....

3 When the film <u>has ended</u>, everyone clapped. ....

4 After I've given my presentation, I <u>go</u> out for a meal to celebrate. ....

5 People should not judge a situation until they <u>will experience</u> it themselves. ....

Answer Key

Progress tests

PROGRESS TEST Units 1–2

1 1 problem 2 affects 3 Although 4 effects 5 percentage 6 As a result 7 especially 8 on the other hand 9 In fact 10 percent

2 1 stressful 2 generally 3 irregular 4 careful 5 healthy 6 easily 7 reasonable 8 inconvenient 9 dramatically 10 fitness

3 1 better 2 less 3 happier 4 more enjoyable 5 hardest 6 more clearly 7 further/farther 8 worse 9 hottest 10 highest

4 1 B 2 C 3 A 4 B 5 C

5 1 to 2 of 3 to 4 to/towards 5 On

PROGRESS TEST Units 3–4

1 1 research 2 data 3 hypothesis 4 experiments 5 laboratory 6 analysis 7 findings 8 journal

2 1 C 2 A 3 B 4 B 5 C 6 B 7 A 8 C

3 1 has been studying 2 have been conducting 3 lived 4 has broken 5 haven't seen 6 spoke

4 1 – 2 – 3 the 4 The 5 – 6 an 7 a 8 the 9 – 10 a

5 1 In/During 2 from 3 by 4 Between 5 at 6 in/during 7 in 8 to

PROGRESS TEST Units 5–6

1 1 solar 2 environment 3 endangered / extinct 4 habitats 5 renewable

2 1 B 2 C 3 A 4 C 5 B 6 C

3 1 retailers 2 assistant 3 choice 4 sales 5 shelves

4 1 c 2 b 3 e 4 a 5 d 6 f

5 1 reached 2 can be used 3 were caused 4 consists 5 was blown 6 fit

6 1 branches 2 get 3 interest 4 balance 5 give 6 debt

7 Everyone knows that retailers, **who** rely on their sales, have to use advertising to promote their products. Unfortunately, as consumers, we have no choice over **when** we see these advertisements or **where** they are placed. No matter **what** we are doing, there seem to be advertisements everywhere.

They often occur on television in the middle of an important scene. Suddenly, your concentration is interrupted by someone **who** is trying to sell you car insurance. When this happens on my television, the volume also increases, **which** really annoys me. I cannot understand **why** this happens!

PROGRESS TEST Units 7–8

1 1 g 2 f 3 b 4 e 5 a 6 c

2 1 aged 2 age group 3 ages 4 age of 5 of age 6 age group

3 1 e 2 g 3 d 4 b 5 f 6 a

4 1 costumes 2 well-known 3 exhibit 4 contemporary 5 mend 6 task

5 1 them 2 ones 3 it 4 others 5 you 6 they

6 1 B 2 B 3 A 4 A 5 C

7 1 go 2 wore 3 ended 4 am going / will go 5 experience / have experienced

Speaking reference

Part 1

Topics and questions

2 k 3 h 4 a 5 g 6 c 7 i 8 e 9 j 10 b
11 f 12 l

Exercise

a Present simple – 1, 4, 5, 6, 7, 10
b Present continuous – 11
c Past simple – 2, 3, 8
d Present perfect – 9, 12

How are you rated?

1 b, e
2 d, g, h
3 a, i
4 c, f, j

Writing reference

Task 1

1 Graphs

1 Total population in billions
2 50 years (2000–2050)
3 It shows past, present and predicted populations for China and India / an increasing trend for India / an increase and decrease for China.
4 Key points: India's population was lower than China's in 2000. / India and China will have the same populations in 2030. / India's population will be higher than China's in 2050.
5 Key points: In 2000, there were more people living in China than in India. / By 2030, both countries will have the same population / 1.45 billion. / China's population is likely to fall slightly to 1.4 billion in 2050, while India's population will probably increase and reach 1.6 billion.
6 Yes, the data is accurate.
7 a […] rise in; has increased by; will increase; is likely to fall slightly; will [probably] increase and reach; experience steady growth in; will overtake; will peak in; begin to fall

2 Pie charts

1 The chart shows percentages of different forms of energy used in the world. The bar on the right shows percentages of different forms of renewable energy.
2 The high percentages of coal, oil and natural gas used. / The small percentages of nuclear power and renewable energy used. / The fact that most renewable energy used is biomass and hydroelectric.

3 *Suggested answers*
§1: introduction; §2: figures for coal, oil and natural gas; §3: figures for renewable energy; §4: overview.
4 Clearly, we are very dependent on these three main energy supplies.
5 The overview is the final paragraph.
6 By far the biggest; Similar but much smaller; are the largest; is the smallest; compared to
7 and; Also; Clearly; Similar; while; In addition; Although

3 Tables and bar charts

1 They are both about internet use; either chart could be summarised first, as one is not dependent on the other.
2 Internet use at different ages; internet use for different purposes
3 A reference to the main differences in age and use
4 §1: introduction; §2: age groups and use; §3: different uses; §4: overview
5 Figures included: 89%, 14–17, 99%, 20–29, 91%, 64, 56, 63%, 62%, 22%; they are included to support key points about age groups and internet use.

4 Diagrams

1 1 storage; 2 separation into steam and gases;
   3 treatment of gases; 4 water vapour and cleaned gases
2 *Suggested answer*
transported / stored / separate / take / cleaned / removed / released
Present simple tense and passive forms
3 Compare: treatment of steam and gas; uses of ash, gas and steam
4 Yes. §1: introduction and overview; §2: waste and storage, products from burn, what happens to ash; §3: final stages
5 When; Eventually; Before; Then; also; Finally
6 arrives; is tipped; can be stored; is needed; is collected; burned; produces; is sent; taken; is used; must be treated; is separated; used to drive; are also cleaned; are released

Task 2

Two questions

1 The use of new words and different forms of spelling and grammar
2 a) The reason why mobile phones and the Internet have changed the way we spell and write, and produced new vocabulary; b) whether I think this is a good or bad thing
3 §2: comparison of old and new technology; §3: effect of speed on the way we write; §4: reason why it's OK and reason why it could be bad

4 and; However; especially; Unfortunately; for example; What is more; Yet; However; All in all; On the other hand

5 The idea of speed

Two opposing views

1 *Suggested answer*
Some people like history, and some people can't see its relevance to today's world.

2 Five views: historians; tourists; people in general; youngsters; the writer

3 §1: introduction + statement of writer's view;
§2: views of historians – people who like history;
§3: views of tourists and other people + example from the writer's experience – people who like history;
§4: views of youngsters – people who dislike history;
§5: conclusion + repetition of writer's view

4 1 other people 2 the past 3 historians 4 beautiful arts and crafts 5 youngsters 6 different things

To what extent do you agree?

1 c

2 One, but you have to take a stand and decide how much you agree or disagree.

3 2 totally 3 matter 4 food 5 subjects 6 topics 7 skills 8 deeply 9 children 10 world
The words in the box are more appropriate; they are less vague and display a wider vocabulary.

4 b; in the first and last paragraphs (but also implied in the writer's arguments)

5 Caring about the environment is really a social *thing*.
Parents encourage it / Schools teach it
Reading and writing, on the other hand, are things that everyone needs.
Learn at school / Needed for job

Practice tests

Listening, Section 1

1 Dress your Best (*capitals optional*)
2 Kirby
3 09356 788 545
4 (extra) charge
5 American Express (*capitals optional*)
6 black/dark
7 Glass desk(s)
8 TG 586
9 yellow
10 Coffee table

W When are they?

M Well, there's one on the 16th of the month, but there's a charge of 40 dollars for that one.

W Oh, that's a lot!

M Mmm. Or there's option 2, which is the end of the month … I'll have to confirm the date later … and that's a free delivery.

W I'll take option 2, thanks, I don't want to pay a charge.

M OK – I'll note that down just in case.

W We haven't organised the office yet, so there should be plenty of time.

M Uh-huh. And lastly, you don't have an account with us … so how would you like to pay?

W Oh – I'll pay by credit card.

M OK – will that be Visa?

W Is American Express OK?

M Absolutely fine.

M So – what would you like to order, Miss Brown?

W Well, I've been looking in your catalogue, and you have some office chairs that look very comfortable for our type of work.

M Is there an item code?

W Yes, it's ASP 23.

M OK – those chairs come in pink, white and black.

W Yes, the pink looks nice, but I think the darker colour's better for us – you can see light materials on it more easily.

M That's true.

W We'll have five of those, I think.

M OK. I've got that. Anything else?

W Do you have any striped mats?

M I'm sorry, not at the moment – they're out of stock. We should have some in next month.

W Never mind. Well, um, I'd also like two of your glass desks.

M They're lovely, aren't they?

W Yes – you seem to have two sizes.

M Basically large or small … I think the code for the small ones is …

W I think we'll have the large ones – the code here is TG 586.

M OK, so that's two glass desks. Any lamps for those?

W No – we have to get special lamps for our work.

M Oh, I see, do you have another supplier for those?

W Yes … um, we do need some furniture for our customers, though.

M OK – for a waiting area or something?

W Well, we have to discuss the work with them, so we need a nice sofa …

M Something soft and …

W I thought leather …

M Ah yes, a good choice.

W There's a three-seater here – DFD 44 – that seems to be in red, cream or chocolate brown.

M Yes, it does come in yellow as well.

W Yellow … Mmm. I'd thought of red … but … that sounds lively – yes, I'll have that colour. I think brown's a bit too dull, and cream shows the dirt too much.

M Yeah, you're right. Anything else? A coffee table, perhaps?

W Yes, I think so. Maybe TX 22, the round, silver one.

M A very good choice.

W Well, that's it, I think.

M OK … I'll just add that up for you and then take your credit-card details …

Listening, Section 2

11 plan
12 on foot
13 sensible clothes
14 (weather) forecast
15 volunteers
16 accidents
17 finish line
18 C
19 B
20 E

Section 2 Recording script   CD2 Track 21

Announcer: Now, we're grateful to Fred McKinnon for coming in to the studio today to give everyone a few tips about the city marathon that's taking place next Saturday …

Fred: Thanks, Shweta. Yes, we're all very excited about the big event. Let me just remind listeners that a marathon is a 26-mile or 42-kilometre race, and this year we have 12,000 runners taking part. So, if you're thinking of going out to support the runners – and I know that many of you are – here are some tips to help make your day more enjoyable.

First of all, be certain to plan ahead. Don't leave everything to the last minute. Many roads are going to be closed – we don't have exact times for these closures yet, but my big advice to you is don't rely on your car to get you anywhere. The marathon route runs through the city centre, so much better to take the bus or the train – though these methods of transport will only go as far as the outskirts of the city. In fact, the best way to get around the town will be on foot. You may choose to cycle, but you still won't be able to go on roads near the runners' route.

Now, we did a broadcast last week in which we told all our runners to wear the right kind of shoes … and I'm going to tell you to put on sensible clothes. A lot of visitors will be coming to the city, you may be hunting for someone in the race that you want to support, the weather may be hot or it may be wet … Which leads me on to another thing – make sure you look at the forecast on Friday night. If it's going to rain, take an umbrella, and if it's going to be hot, take some drinks. However, please don't try to pass these to the runners. We already have hundreds of volunteers, who'll be standing on the roadside doing just that.

When you get into the town, find yourself a spot to stand in … you may well want to walk up and down the route, but please don't cross the road. There could be thousands of people running towards you, some very tired and not able to focus clearly. We don't want any accidents, and runners don't want obstacles like you in their path. What they do need is your support – particularly when their energies are low – so cheer them on, and for once, don't worry about noise! The louder, the better.

Lastly, if you have friends or relatives who're taking part in the run, please don't say that you'll see them at the finish line. If everyone does that, the whole area will be terribly congested, and you won't be able to find anyone. Well, that's most of the advice …

Now, I mentioned transport earlier and I've just got a few more bits of information about travel on the day.

As I said earlier, roads in the town centre will be closed, but if you need to be picked up at your home, then you could take a taxi some of the way. Unlike the trams and trains, however, they'll be held up on the roads, so passengers shouldn't expect them to be as punctual as they normally are. Don't be put off by this, though – there'll be extra drivers working that day, and you'll get one eventually.

Um, if you're meeting up with friends and want to be around when the runners set off (that's 9 am, by the way), whatever end of the city you're coming from, I'd say use the trams. They still have routes that cross roads, and this will inevitably lead to some problems, but they're likely to have more reliable timetables than buses at this time of day and, as you know, unlike taxis, they can carry plenty of passengers.

Lastly, the buses. Quite a number of bus routes will be altered slightly, and it's already been decided that some will be closed. There won't be fewer drivers, but they will be operating on different routes and some will have longer breaks than they normally do. We'll be including a full list of all the bus routes and numbers and where they'll be going in this week's local paper, so look out for that.

Well, that's it from me. Back to you, Shweta.

A Thanks very much, Fred.

Listening, Section 3

21 C
22 B
23 A
24 C
25 A
26 B
27 D/E
28 E/D
29 A/C
30 C/A

Section 3 Recording script CD2 Track 22

Tutor: Come in!

Ahmed: Hi.

T Oh, hello Ahmed … how are you?

A Fine, thanks.

T Have a seat. So … how do you think the seminar went last week?

A Oh, well … I enjoyed it, yes, though I'm not sure I really followed parts of the discussion that took place, you know, about the theory and all that …

T Well, we can talk about that later … but were you comfortable in a group?

A Oh, it's better, I think, than working on your own – though you're comparing yourself all the time with the other students there.

T OK, well, let's talk about how you did and look at some strategies to help you in the future.

A That would be great.

T Now, one of the things that students often overlook when they go to seminars is that you do need to prepare for them. You can't rely on other people.

A I know, and I did look at the results of the experiments we did in class and try to analyse them beforehand … as you said.

T Yes … and that was good. But you have to do some background reading as well. Did you get the list of articles I sent round?

A Mmm – I've started to read them …

T OK, well, you'll know that for next time.

A Yes, sure.

T So let's move on to your participation in the seminar.

A Right.

T Perhaps you can tell me how you think that went?

A Yeah, well, I'm not used to talking to more than a couple of people – it's very different from the way we learn in my home country.

T Yes, I appreciate that.

A So I think I, um … well, I know I should have included everyone, but I think I kept turning to the person next to me.

T Is that because you were avoiding eye contact?

A I don't think so – I'm not shy – it's just habit, I think.

T Well, that will improve as we do more seminars.

A Uh-huh.

T Um, another difficulty is knowing when to speak.

A Like when it's your turn?

T Yes.

A I felt I did wait for a pause …

T Yes, you handled that quite well.

A The thing I'm really concerned about is keeping up with the discussion.

T Does your mind wander off?

A Sometimes. I jot down a lot of information, but I still find myself thinking about something else when lots of other students are talking.

T Mmm. If there's an assignment to do at the end of the seminar, that usually helps!

A I'm sure it does.

T OK, now, the last thing I want to look at is the role that you play in the seminar.

A What do you mean?

T Well, when students work in groups, they don't all behave the same way. Some students are quiet, some look for support, some ask a lot of questions ….

A Oh … that's a new idea to me. I don't know what I'm like …

T That's probably because you're thinking about your own performance all the time.

A I guess so. I mean, should I be different in some way?

T What I would say is that when we do the next seminar, you should look more at the people around you … you know, look outside yourself.

A Like, ask myself how they feel?

T Yes, or what they're looking for from the group.

A OK.

T It doesn't take much, but it's important to watch what other students are doing.

A OK. I'll do that.

T Fine. Now, …

T Now, I'm going to suggest a couple of strategies for next week's seminar.

A OK – that's great. I need to participate more.

T Well, it's not a question of saying more – but we need everyone to feel comfortable about giving their views.

A Then the discussion is better.

T Yes. So … you're a confident person …

A Should I make sure I'm near someone who's quiet?

T You can do, but it's more about how well you pay attention to other students.

A OK – so I need to be attentive.

T Yes, and then encourage someone else to say more by saying: What did you mean when you said … or What do you think about the idea that …

A That way I'm talking …

T Yes, but you'll find that other people will talk, too. You'll all start to get really involved.

A Right – they're good suggestions.

T The other thing that can really help is the way you take notes.

A Yeah, I know I write down everything, but I should be stricter with myself.

T Well, you actually need to think a few days ahead.

A Really?

T Yes – 'What's the topic?' and 'What's the best way of making notes?'

A I see. So I have a strategy when I walk in the room.

T Exactly. Then, when you read them through later, they'll make sense and you won't have to write them out again.

A I always have to do that!

T The other thing I would say is that you should include a small column in your notes where you can jot down things you want to go back to before the seminar ends.

A Like a reminder.

T Yes. Notes aren't just for later – you can use them as a prompt when there's a pause in the discussion.

A That's been really helpful.

T OK – see you in class tomorrow.

A Thanks.

Listening, Section 4

31 rain shadow
32 few inches
33 (other) minerals
34 collect
35 (green) stem
36 expand
37 white hairs
38 (sharp) thorns
39 (very) tough
40 plastic

Section 4 Recording script   CD2 Track 23

In today's lecture, I'm going to continue our work on plants and talk about plants that live in the desert. Now, just a bit of background information first. As you know, about a third of the world is covered in desert, and the sort of area they're found in is important. Deserts are usually created because the area of land where they lie is located in something that's called a 'rain shadow'. Now, this is a region that's beneath a mountain range, um, and what happens is that the wind blows over the mountains towards the area, but as it does so, the air loses its moisture and becomes very dry.

Because of this 'downwind' location, rainfall often totals just a few inches a year or, in some regions, there's absolutely none. And you can imagine the effect of this … It means that whatever rain does fall evaporates quickly from the ground, and that makes the soil salty … and also leaves behind a whole range of other minerals as well.

Now, despite this, deserts are home to many living things. In fact, they're second only to tropical rainforests in the variety of plant and animal species that live there.

So, how do plants grow in a place that's so dry? Well, they're specially adapted to do this. In fact, many of the fascinating features of desert plants are adaptations – these are traits that help the plant survive in its harsh environment. And desert plants have two main adaptations: the first is that they have an ability to collect water and then to store it. Some have large root systems and amazing internal water-storage systems. The second adaptation is that they have features that can actually reduce water loss … and these are often very special leaf designs or additions to the plant structure.

So let's have a look at some examples. Desert plants often look very different from any other plants …

OK. This first one is the Saguaro Cactus, which grows in North America. It looks a bit like an open hand with long fingers. This plant has a large network of roots that extend far, far away from its trunk, and these roots collect water after rain, and that's taken here to the green stem. This is where all its water is kept, and it keeps the whole plant alive until the next rain comes. It's a pretty, woody plant – in fact, um, its skeleton is actually used in building materials, so it's quite strong.

This next plant is called the Barrel Cactus – named because it does look rather like a barrel. It can grow up to a metre in height, which is pretty big, and it has long, yellow spines. Now, this plant has an interesting adaptation because its shape allows it to expand when it rains – hence the barrel – and store water in its spongy tissue. But then it shrinks in size during dry times as it uses the stored water. So that's a clever design.

This third cactus – often just one plant reaching upwards – has these white hairs all over its surface. It's called the Old Man Cactus because of the white hairs, and these help the plant reflect the hot desert sun. So this adaptation is a water conservation aid if you like.

Another adaptation not directly connected with water but with survival is found on something like the Prickly Pear Cactus. There are hundreds of these in the Mexican desert. I'm sure you've seen them on films and adverts … Um, yes, so because desert plants store water in their spongy tissue, animals will eat them. So the plant has sharp thorns specially designed to prevent the predator from being able to – well, get near it at all.

Our next plant is called the Desert Spoon. This plant has long leaves that fan out, and they're very succulent because they can also store water inside. However, they're also usually very tough, and this helps keep the water inside and also makes them less tasty.

Finally, we come to the Aloe Plant. This is one that many people keep in their homes. It's an attractive plant which has leaves that look and feel rather waxy. This surface behaves in a similar way to a plastic wrapper and helps the plant to hold the water in. It's a wonder plant, this one. Its juice has been used as a medicine for centuries, and even today, you can find it in products on the pharmacists' shelves or in creams and lotions.

OK … well, we're going to take a closer look …

Reading, Passage 1

1 TRUE
2 FALSE
3 TRUE
4 TRUE
5 NOT GIVEN
6 FALSE
7 (a) wire
8 solar power
9 (an) inflatable dummy
10 a mark
11 (an) extending arm
12 navigation
13 two(-)way communication

Reading, Passage 2

14 D
15 E
16 A
17 F
18 A
19 G
20 C/D
21 D/C
22 B/C
23 C/B
24 forest footprint
25 decaying plants
26 60%

Reading Passage 3

27 C
28 B
29 A
30 D
31 B
32 YES
33 NO
34 YES
35 YES
36 NOT GIVEN
37 D
38 G
39 C
40 A

Writing Task 1

Sample answer

The data show how people felt about the service provided by US airlines between 1999 and 2007.

Firstly, the graph indicates that general satisfaction levels rose slightly, from 65 percent in 1999 to 72 percent in 2007, while the percentage of dissatisfied customers fell to 24 percent over the same period.

According to the table, customers were most satisfied with the politeness of airline staff and plane schedules, and least satisfied with the seating. Data provided for 2007 show that only 47 percent of travellers felt the seats were comfortable. In contrast, satisfaction with staff remained fairly stable at about 90 percent over the eight-year period, and rose in the case of schedules from 75 to 79 percent. However, the biggest increase in satisfaction was in connection with ticket prices, where figures rose by 20 percent to 65 percent in 2007.

Overall it can be seen that levels of satisfaction were quite high throughout the period, and customers were most satisfied with the service from staff.

(174 words)

Writing Task 2

Sample answer

We all need healthy food every day, but it is particularly important for children to eat well because their bodies are still growing.

Most people agree that it is difficult to learn anything if you are hungry because the brain needs food in order to function well. Studies have shown that children who are hungry have trouble concentrating and become slow learners. In addition, the school day can be quite long and involve many activities. Teachers cannot expect children to participate fully if they have an empty stomach.

Many children do eat something at school, even if it is only a snack. However, some snacks are not very nutritious. Crisps and chips, for example, are very fatty and contain a lot of salt, while biscuits are sugary. Although these food items may increase energy levels, they only have a short-term effect. A healthy meal, on the other hand, will keep energy levels higher for longer and help children learn more easily.

In my view, it is up to parents and schools to make sure that children eat healthily. Schools may provide meals, but if parents prefer to decide what their children eat, there needs to be a choice. In my country, children can either have a school meal, which they pay for, or bring a packed lunch. I think this is a good system, but in other countries a different system may be preferable.

In conclusion, a healthy meal will definitely help children to study more successfully. However, both parents and schools have a responsibility to make sure that this is provided for them.

(264 words)

Acknowledgements

David Jay would like to thank the following people for
all their support: the editorial team at CUP, his friends,
and his family, especially his father, Jeffrey Jay.

The authors and publishers are grateful to the following
contributors:

Editor: Andrew Reid

Lexicographer: Elizabeth Walter

Proofreader: Kevin Doherty

Picture researcher: Diane Jones

Illustrations Wild Apple Design Ltd

Cover design by David Lawton

Designed and typeset by Wild Apple Design Ltd